The Cultural Side of Islam

BY

MUHAMMAD MARMADUKE PICKTHALL.

KITAB BHAVAN
New Delhi-110002

KITAB BHAVAN
Exporters & Importers
1784, Kalan Mahal, Daryaganj
New Delhi- 110002. (India)
Phones: 3274686, 263383
Telex No. 31-63106 ALI IN

First Published in India 1927
3rd. Edition   1990

ISBN 81-7151-094-9

Published by:
Nusrat Ali Nasri for Kitab Bhavan
1784, Kalan Mahal, Daryaganj
New Delhi- 110002

Printed in India :
at Chaman offset Printer
1626,Sui Walan
New Delhi-110002

PREFACE.

The Committee of "Madras Lectures on Islam" has great pleasure in presenting to the public the second series of Lectures delivered at Madras in January last by Mr. Muhammad Marmaduke Pickthall on "the Cultural Side of Islam." In October 1925 the first series of Lectures were delivered in Urdu by Moulana Syed Suleiman Sahib Nadvi on "The Life of the Holy Prophet" which has been published. In the lectures on "Islamic Culture" Mr. Pickthall has vividly portrayed the true picture of Islam and has clearly described the causes for the rise and decline of Islamic Culture. These lectures, resplendent with important quotations from the Holy Quran and the Traditions of the Holy Prophet, breathe the real spirit of Islam appealing both to the soul and the intellect.

The Committee feels that the lectures, when read by the public, will not only be appreciated, but will really serve the great need of understanding the true Islamic Religion and its Culture. The Committee offers its warm thanks to the learned lecturer and to the distinguished Chairman of the inaugural meeting, the Hon'ble Sir C. P. Ramaswami Ayyar.

THE COMMITTEE OF
"MADRAS LECTURES ON ISLAM."
16, *Thambu Chetty Street,*

Madras, 11th *July* 1927.

CONTENTS.

CONTENTS

FIRST LECTURE.

Islamic Culture.

Culture means cultivation and, as the word is generally used now-a-days when used alone, especially the cultivation of the human mind. Islamic culture differs from other cultures in that it can never be the aim and object of the cultivated individual, since its aim, clearly stated and set before every one, is not the cultivation of the individual or group of individuals, but of the entire human race. No amount of works of art, or works of literature, in any land can be regarded as the justification of Islam so long as wrong, injustice and intolerance remain. No victories of war or peace, however brilliant, can be quoted as he harvest of Islam. Islam has wider objects, grander views. It aims at nothing less than universal human brotherhood. Still, as a religion, it does encourage human effort after self- and race-improvement more than any other religion and since it became a Power in the world, it has produced cultural results which will bear comparison with the results achieved by all the other religions, civilizations and philosophies put together. A Muslim can only be astonished at the importance, almost amounting to worship, ascribed to works of art and literature—which one may call the incidental phenomena of culture—in the West; as if they were the justification, and their production the highest aim, of human life. Not that Muslims despise or ever should despise, literary, artistic and scientific achievements; but that they regard them in the light of blessings by the way; either as aids to the end or refreshment for the wayfarer. They do not idolise the aid and the refreshment.

The whole of Islam's great work in science, art and literature is included under these two heads—aid and refreshment. Some of it, such as the finest poetry and architecture, falls under both. All of it recognises one leader, follows one guidance, looks towards one Goal. The leader is the Prophet (صلعم), the guidance is the Holy Quran, and the Goal is Allah.

By Islamic culture, I mean not the culture, from whatever source derived, attained at any given moment by people who profess the religion of Islam, but the kind of culture prescribed by a religion of which human progress is the definite and avowed aim.

No one who has ever studied the Quran will deny that it promises success *in this world* and hereafter to men who act upon its guidance and obey its laws; that it aims at nothing less than the success of mankind as a whole; and that this success is to be attained by cultivation of man's gifts and faculties.

If any development in Muslim society is not sanctioned by the Quran or some express injunction of the Prophet, it is un-Islamic and its origin must be sought outside the Islamic polity. The Muslims cannot expect success from their adoption of it, though it need not necessarily militate against success. If any development is contrary to an express injunction of the Quran, and against the teaching and example of the Prophet, then it is anti-Islamic; it must militate against success, and Muslims simply court disaster by adopting it.

Certain art-forms were discouraged by Islam at the beginning, because of their association with the idolatrous worship of the pagan Arabs and its vicious orgies, the utter extirpation of which was necessary for the progress of the race; but the discouragement of certain art expressions and encouragement of others were both, like the works of art produced, regarded as subsidiary. The culture of Islam aimed not at beautifying and refining the accessories of human life. It aimed at beautifying and exalting human life itself. There is to-day a large and undoubtedly intellectual school of thought in the West which seems to hold that the production of fine works of art by a small minority of a community is sufficient reason for acclaiming the civilization and culture of that community, even though the huge majority of its members may be forced by the social order under which they live to lead ugly and degraded lives—nay, there is an intellectual school of thought which seems to hold that the production of fine works of art by a minority of any nation is sufficient justification for condemning the majority to conditions of perpetual ugliness, servitude and degradation.

Some of you will, no doubt, remember a discussion in the English Press some years ago. The question was this : Suppose a famous and very beautiful Greek statue, unique of its kind and therefore irreplaceable, is in the same room with a living baby, and the room catches fire; it is only possible to save one or the other: which should be saved? Very many correspondents, men of intellect and good position—I remember—held that the statue should be saved and the child left to perish; their argument being that millions of babies are born every day, whereas that masterpiece of old Greek art could never be replaced. That is a view no Muslim could have taken —the very latest, cultivated form of idol-worship.

Islam foresees, and works for, a radiant future for the human race; and though every Muslim holds his own life cheap in the service of Allah, which is the service of humanity, he would never dream of sacrificing any human life, however insignificant seeming, to the work of human hands. The adoration—it amounts to that—of works of art is due to disbelief in Allah's guidance and His purpose for mankind. These things are the best that man has produced in the centuries; beauty is decreasing, human beings are deteriorating—so runs the argument— therefore, we must cling to these beautiful productions of the past as the one ideal left to us. That is pessimism, and Islam is optimistic—optimistic not with the " optimism " satirised by Voltaire in the character of Dr. Pangloss, the absurd philosopher, who kept exclaiming " Tout est pour le mieux dans le meilleur des mondes possibles." (All is for the best in this best of possible worlds.) That is the kind of remark which passes with the unthinking for optimism, but it is really fata ism— which is a form of pessimism; and Islam is not fatalistic.

Yes, I repeat that statement. In spite of all that has been said and written of the fatalism of the Muslims Islam is not fatalistic in the generally accepted meaning of the word. It does not bid man accept the existing conditions as a necessary evil, but commands him never to cease striving for improvement.

Islam is a religion which specifically aims at human progress, and shows the proper way of it in a number of commands and prohibitions covering every avocation of man's daily life, his social life and politics as well as every prompting of his mind and spirit. These commands and prohibitions have been codified into a complete social and political system. It is a practicable system, for it has been practised with a success which is the great astonishment of history. Many writers have tried to explain away the amazing success of Islam by ascribing it to outside causes—weakness of the surrounding nations, free use of the sword, the credulity of the times, and so forth. But how would they explain away the fact that so long as the Muslims implicitly obeyed a particular injunction of the Sacred Law they succeeded in the sphere of that injunction, and whenever they neglected to obey it failed; and how would they explain the fact that any non-Muslims, doing what the Muslims are enjoined to do, have always succeeded in that special direction, except by the supposition that the injunctions of the Quran and the Holy Prophet are laws for all mankind—natural laws which men transgress at their peril, or rather at the peril of the race ? It was because those laws could not be found out by individual experiment, and could only partly be detected in the long run of history by a student and a thinker here and there, that they required to be revealed by a Prophet. Otherwise they are as natural as the physical laws which govern our existence evidently and which none would dream of disputing.

Other religions promise success in another life to those who qualify themselves for it by privation and austerity on earth. Islam promises success and fruition in this life—just as much as in the other—to all men, if they will but obey certain laws and plain rules of conduct. The division between this world and the other vanishes for the true Muslim, since Allah is the Lord of the Heavens and the Earth, the Sovereign of this world just as much as of the others. The other life has its beginning now, and not at death, for all who perform the act of Al-Islam—that Self-Surrender to the Will of God which the Holy Prophet meant when he advised us :

موتوا قبل ان تموتوا .

"Die before you die."

The success in this world promised by Islam is not the success of one human being at the expense of others, nor of one nation to the detriment and despair of others, but the success of mankind as a whole. Five times a day, from every mosque in the world, the call goes forth

حي علي الفلاح ! حي علي الفلاح .

"Come to falah! Come to falah!" The Arabic word "falâh" means success through cultivation. And there is another Arabic word, in common use among Muslims, of which the original meaning is often forgotten in its technical application: زكوة meaning, "cultivation by pruning," "causing to grow straight." It is the name given to the Islamic poor-rate, so frequently enjoined in the Quran as a duty equal to worship, which truly was a cause of cultivated growth to the community.

"A tax shall be taken from the rich and given to the poor," said the Prophet (May God bless and keep him). When that tax was regularly collected the condition of Muslim society became such that, though the dispensers of زكاة sought far and wide, no proper objects of زكاة—that is, destitute and ignorant Muslims—could be found and the money was expended upon works of public benefit.

In the Holy Quran we read:

$$قد افلح من زكيها$$
$$وقد خاب من دسيها .$$

"He is indeed successful who causeth it (the human soul) to grow aright,

And he is indeed a failure who stunteth and starveth it."

And again

$$قد افلح من تزكي$$
$$وذكر اسم ربه فصلى .$$

"He is successful who groweth

And remembereth the name of his Lord, so prayeth."

Some may think that these are mere religious aspirations and expressions apart from life. Islam is nothing if not practical, and the expressions have been no dead letter in Islam, since they were translated practically into a system of organised relief and charity upon the grandest scale ever attempted, and solved all social problems in the Muslim world for centuries. The Quran informs us that true religion is practical, not *theoretical* or formal.

ليس البر ان تولوا وجوهكم قبل المشرق والمغرب
ولكن البر من آمن بالله واليوم الآخر والملائكة والكتاب
والنبيين وآتى ماله على حبه ذوى القربى واليتامى
والمساكين وابن السبيل والسائلين وفي الرقاب واقام الصلوة
وآتى الزكوة والموفون بعهدهم اذا عهدوا والصابرين
في البأساء والضراء وحين البأس اولئك الذين صدقوا
واولئك هم المتقون ۰

"It is not righteousness that ye turn your faces to the East and the West, but righteous is he who believeth in Allah and the Last Day and the Angels and the Scripture and the Prophets, and giveth his wealth for love of Him to kindred and to orphans and to the needy and the homeless and to beggars and to set slaves free; and those who are regular in prayer and pay the poor their legal portion. And those who keep their promise when they make one, and the persevering in adversity and tribulation. These are they who are sincere. These are they who keep from evil."

الذين آمنوا وعملوا الصالحات ۰

"Those who believe and do good."

How often does that phrase occur in the Holy Quran. "Those who believe and do nothing" cannot exist in Islam. "Those who believe and do wrong" are inconceivable, for Islam means man's surrender to God's will, and so obedience to His Law which is a law of effort not of idleness.

There was no distinction between secular education and religious education in the great days of Islam. All education was brought into the religious sphere. To quote a recent European writer: "It was the glory of Islam that it gave to other sciences the same footing which it gave to the study of the Quran and the Hadith and Fiqh (that is, Muslim Jurisprudence), a place in the Mosque." Lectures on chemistry and physics, botany, medicine and astronomy were given in the mosque equally with lectures on the above-named subjects; for the Mosque was the University of Islam in the great days, and it deserved the name of University, since it welcomed to its precincts all the knowledge of the age from every quarter. It was this unity and exaltation of all learning which gave to the old Muslim writers that peculiar quality which every reader of them must have noticed, the calm serenity of orbed minds.

In Islam, there are no such terms as secular and religious, for true religion includes the whole sphere of man's activities. The distinction drawn in the Holy Quran is between good, that which is helpful to man's growth, and evil, that which is detrimental and noxious to it. Islam is a rational religion. It has no place for the man who can say, with St. Augustine: "Credo quia absurdum est "—"I believe *because* it is incredible." Again and again does the Quran denounce irrational religion as religion evidently false. Again and again does it appeal to men to use their reason and especially their common sense in matters of religion. All historical experience goes to prove that a large measure of free

1-A

thought is absolutely necessary to human progress, and
at the same time that nations which lose faith in God
deteriorate. Are the two things, the living faith in God
and the large measure of free thought, incompatible ?

A considerable school of thought in the West seems
to think that they are incompatible. Islam has proved
that they are perfectly compatible. In the early, the
successful centuries of Islam, an intense faith in God
was combined with free thought upon every earthly
subject : for Islam held nothing upon earth so sacred as
to be immune from criticism. There was only One
Supernatural, only One Incomprehensible, Whose Unity,
having been once accepted, admitted of no further discussion. He was One for all, Beneficent and Merciful
towards all alike, and He had bestowed on man the gift
of reason, which is extolled by Muslim writers as the
highest gift, to be used quite freely in the name of Allah—
that is to say, with the purpose of pursuing what is good
and eschewing what is evil, for which the Sacred Law
affords guidance and safeguards. There is no priesthood in Islam. All the prerogatives and responsibilities
which in other religions have been arrogated to a priesthood, in the system of Islam are vested in the individual
human mind. So the most wise and learned men became
the natural leaders

Since an unenlightened mind would be a sorry lamp
to light the steps of any man or woman, this exaltation
of reason carried with it the command for universal
education. The Prophet himself said :

طلب العلم فريضة على كل مسلم وكل مسلمة .

"To seek knowledge is a duty for every Muslim (male)
and every Muslimah (female)." Universal education
both for men and women thus became the Sacred Law
of Islam thirteen centuries before it was adopted by the
civilization of the West. He also is reported to have said
(though the saying is not well authenticated): "Seek
knowledge though it be in China"; and the following well-
authenticated saying shows the importance not only of
acquiring knowledge but of spreading knowledge among
the people:

اِن اللہ لایقبض العلم انتزاعاً ینتزعہ عن العباد ولکن
یقبض العلم بقبض العلماء حتی اذالم یبقی عالماً اتخذ
الناس رؤسا جهالًا فسئلوا فافتوا بغیر علم فضلوا واضلوا .

"Verily Allah doth not keep knowledge as a thing
apart that he withholdeth from His servants, but he doth
keep it in the grasp of men of knowledge, so that if he
shall cause not a man of knowledge to remain, mankind
will take foolish heads, and they will be questioned and
give fatwas, and they will err and lead others into error."
The picture is too clearly of the present condition of Islam,
when we have plenty of narrow theologians, for us to
doubt but that the meaning of the word knowledge as
here used is something wider and more human than the
knowledge they possess.

He said: "The ink of the scholar is more holy than
the blood of the martyr." He said: "An hour's contemplation and study of God's creation is better than a
year of adoration."

He said: "He dieth not who seeketh knowledge."
"Whosoever revereth the learned, revereth me." "The

first thing created was reason." "Allah hath not created anything better than reason. The benefits which Allah giveth are on account of it, and understanding is by it; and Allah's displeasure is caused by it, and by it are rewards and punishments." He said: "To listen to the words of the learned and to instil into others the lessons of science is better than religious exercises."

"He who leaveth his home in search of knowledge, walketh in the path of Allah."

"Acquire knowledge. It enableth the possessor to distinguish right from wrong; it lighteth up the path to Heaven. It is our friend in the desert, our society in solitude, our companion when friendless. It guideth to happiness, it sustaineth in adversity. It is an ornament among friends, and an armour against enemies."

اِن الملائكتة لتضع اجنحتها لطالب العلم ۰

"Lo! the angels offer their wings to the seeker of knowledge."

هل يستوي الذين يعلمون والذين لايعلمون ۰

"Are those who have knowledge on an equality with those who have no knowledge?"

فضل العالم على العابد كفضلى على ادناكم ۰

"The preferment of the learned man above the devotee is as my preferment above the lowest of you."

He said that a man may have performed prayers, fasting, alms-giving, pilgrimage and all other religious duties, but he will be rewarded only in proportion to the common sense which he employed. And he said that he who has learning but knows not how to apply it to the conduct of life is "like a donkey carrying books."

Neither the Holy Quran nor the Holy Prophet ever contemplated the existence of an ignorant Muslim. Indeed, "ignorant Muslim" is a contradiction in terms. In the great days of Islam, an ignorant Muslim, like an indigent Muslim, could hardly have been found.

Islam brought religion back into its proper sphere of action, which is daily life. The light of Allah, spoken of in the Quran, is known to everyone who follows Allah's guidance, for it is the light of every day transfigured and glorified by the knowledge of His immanence. The aim of religion is no far distant object, situated in a future life; it is present here and now, in service of our fellow-men. The idolators of Arabia kept asking the Holy Prophet for some miracle that might enforce the truth of what he said :

وقالـوا مـا لهذا الرسـول ياكل الطـعـام ويمشي
في الاسواق لولا انزل اليه ملك فيكون معه نذيرا .
او يلقي عليه كنزا و تكـون لـ جنته ياكل منهـا وقال
الظالمون أن تتبعون الا رجلاً مسحورا .

"And they say : What manner of a messenger of God is this who eats food and walks in the bazaars ? Why is not an angel sent down to be a warner with him ?

"Or (why is not) a treasure bestowed on him ? (Or why) hath he not a paradise from which to eat ? The evil-doers say : Ye are but following a man bewitched."

And Allah answered the evil-doers in words which plainly show that miracles are not a proof of the divine messenger, who must appeal to men's reason, not their senses or their curiosity.

وما ارسلنا قبلك من المرسلين الا انهم لياكلون الطعام ويمشون في الاسواق .

"We sent not before thee any messengers but such as verily did eat food and walk in the bazaars."

That is to say, all those Prophets of old of whom the people thought as super-natural beings had been men appealing to the minds of others in God's name.

Miracles, according to the teaching of Islam, are not the proof of divinity, much less do they violate the laws of nature which are themselves divine, being ordained of God. They are evidences of a certain stage of human progress towards the Goal, at which laws hidden from the multitude become apparent. Many miracles are related of Muhammad (God bless him!) but no Muslim would think of quoting them as a proof of his divine mission. The message and the work achieved—the Quran and the Holy Prophet's preaching, and their consequences —speak for themselves, and are above all miracles.

It is, of course, a fact that the majority of professed Muslims are ignorant and superstitious to-day, accepting a vast mass of legends and absurd beliefs; but where man's mind is so exalted in the standing orders of the community, vain beliefs are always threatened with the sword of scepticism. Indeed a large proportion of this mass of legend and superstition merely represents the science of a by-gone day. The spirit of Islam expects it to be superseded by the science of to-day; for the Muslim's mind is free in all affairs of earth, provided that he complies with certain rules of conduct imposed with a view to his bodily, mental and spiritual health ; and it is his duty to explore the science of his day, and to accept what his mind approves of it—aye, even though it dissipates beliefs or fancies long accepted among Muslims. It cannot touch his creed :. " There is no God except Allah, and Muhammad is the Messenger of Allah "—a creed which that grand old sceptic, Gibbon, pronounced to be " composed of an eternal truth and a necessary fiction." Even he had to confess that the " fiction " had been justified in the historic sequel.

There is a great and growing tendency in the Muslim brotherhood to distinguish once for all between the living body of Islamic teaching and the folklore which has been thrown about it like a garment of an antique fashion. How little the discrimination of the robe affects the faith will astonish only those critics, who, misled by the practice of Christianity, have *identified* the latter with the former ; which Muslims never did.

In the Quran, men are bidden to observe the phenomena of nature, the alternation of day and night, the properties of earth and air and fire and water, the mysteries of birth and death, growth and decay—evidences of a law and order which man never made and which man can never bend or alter by a hair's breadth—as proof that man is not the sovereign of this world ; his province of free-will, research and fruitful effort is but a delegated power within an absolute sovereignty ; which absolute sovereignty belongs to Allah, the Creator and Sustainer of the Universe, the Lord of all the Worlds. Man does

not, as a rule, realise the marvels of his natural condition
and of the providence surrounding him, because they
never fail him. Surrounded by a wonder of creative
energy which never fails : placed in a universe subject
to a code of laws which are never broken; manifestly
subject, being unable to inhale a breath, or lift a finger.
or speak a word or think a thought without obeying laws
he never made ; man in general thinks but little of such
matters, absorbed in the interests of his own restricted
sphere of energy, like any insect. Idolising his own
restricted sphere, he looks for a providence which will
back him in his special aims, oblivious of the needs of the
whole creation and of the purpose of the Creator.

Obviously, if we admit that there is a Creator and a
purpose, we must not expect special treatment, but must
seek to conform to the divine will and purpose in creation ;
then only can we hope for success.

كلا إن الانسان ليطغى
ان راء ه استغنى
ان الى ربك الرجعي .

" Nay, verily man is rebellious
" That he deemeth himself independent
" Verily unto thy Lord is the return."

Some years ago there appeared a book written by a
Scottish divine—not a very interesting book—which made
a little stir in the English-speaking world. It was called
"The Natural Law in the Spiritual World." I only
mention it on account of the title, because the revelation
of Islam might be more aptly described as: "The

Natural Law in the Spiritual world and in the Social world and in the Political world." It is to the natural laws which govern man's physical existence that Islam appeals for proof of Allah's actual Kingship, and then goes on to show how laws precisely similar govern man's spiritual and collective life. All the miracles related of all the Prophets and saints are held so unimportant that belief in them is not obligatory. All that is obligatory is belief in Allah's universal sovereignty and in the mission of Muhammad (may God bless and keep him!) and all other Prophets as His human messengers. It was this natural and reasonable basis of Islam which made the greatest of German poets, Goethe, exclaim, after reading a translation of the Quran : If this is Islam, then every thinking man among us is, in fact, a Muslim.

A section—the most vocal section—of the modern world would make objection to Islamic Culture on the ground that it is unsuitable to modern thought and conditions, being founded on the principle, not of democracy or aristocracy or plutocracy—or any other of the systems which have been tried in modern times, and, one may add, have, every one of them, been found wanting—but is founded on the principle of pure theocracy. Not a remote ideal of theocracy, to be contemplated only at hours of worship and forgotten at all other hours ; but an actual, practical, complete theocracy acknowledged and obeyed at all times. A great European statesman is credited with having said : " The Almighty has no part in practical politics," and the chief defect in European politics is, evidently to those who study recent history, that it makes no allowance for the unforeseen event, the Act of God, upsetting careful plans. Allah's law of consequences still operates: the consequence of good is still good, and the consequence of evil, evil in the long run, however much men shut their eyes to the fact. The Russian Revolution and the failure of the Greek attempt upon the life of Turkey are two out of many instances, in our own time, of the unforeseen event, the act of God, frustrating projects of ambition, well-laid plans of statesmen, which seemed humanly speaking to be certain of success.

Indeed, to me, it seems that, as regards the Kingdom of Allah as preached and, to some extent, established by Islam, the position of the modern world is not at all different from that of the mediaeval world. The objectors simply argue on a false analogy. Because the ideal of theocracy which prevailed in Europe in the Middle Ages happened to be associated with miraculous legends and Church ceremonies and regarded as a refuge from a wicked world, these people postulate that all theocracy must be unpractical, a hermit's or fanatic's dream. Miracles have been discredited by modern science, and men have come to think of the exploitation of the riches of this world and of the improvement of their own position in it as a duty. The best think less of improving their own condition, than of improving the condition of their fellowmen. Thus an ideal of theocracy based on the miraculous, and so remote from actual human needs: which was in its very nature pessimistic, regarding this world as the devil's province and bidding all who sought salvation flee from it, may truly be regarded as antiquated and unsuitable to modern circumstances. Not so an ideal of theocracy based upon the natural and the actual. Such an ideal is the crying need of modern life to check its suicidal selfishness—an ideal of which the foundations cannot be shaken by the discoveries of science or the thought of man, for they are in nature itself. The greater the wonders of the natural world as revealed by the progressive work of science, the more triumphantly is Allah's Majesty and Providence and Sovereignty made clear to the true Muslim. So long as the natural laws stand firm, and certain consequences, good or evil, follow certain acts of men and nations, so long must stand the need for man to recognise in human life a higher will and purpose than his own, and to expect a higher judgment than his own; so long must stand the need of man's surrender to that higher will and purpose—which is Islam, as the Quran teaches— if he would succeed.

Islam offers a complete political and social system as an alternative to socialism, fascism, syndicalisms, bolshevism and all the other ' isms ' offered as alternative, to a system which is manifestly threatened with extinction. The system of Islam has the great advantage over all those nostrums, that it has been practised with success —the greater the success the more complete the practice. Every Muslim believes that it must eventually be adopted in its essentials by all nations whether as Muslims or non-Muslims in the technical sense, because its laws are the natural (or divine) laws which govern human progress, and men without the revelation of them, must find their way to them in course of time and painfully, after trying every other way and meeting failure. The system of Islam promises peace and stability where now we see the strife of classes and of nations, and nothing steadfast. It would surely be mere folly on the part of any one to refuse even to study the advantages or disadvantages of such a system merely because it is a system founded on the thought of God, and claiming to have been revealed by a Messenger of God. That would be sheer bigotry of atheism.

But it is not only because it is theocratic that the Islamic system of human culture is despised. It is because of the position and conduct of the Muslims in the world to-day and yesterday and for many yesterdays Christendom in the Middle Ages could not consider it because Christendom was then in bondage to the priests who then, as to-day, called Muhammad (may God bless him!) "the false Prophet", and would not allow anyone even to think that his religion might hold anything good and useful to man-kind : and the tradition of war between the followers of the two religions has been a mighty barrier until the present time, perpetuating intolerance. To-day, when the barrier is practically down, the position of the Muslims in the world is not such as to lead outsiders to suppose that such men know the secret of the way of human progress. The conduct and condition of the Muslims now is a very bad advertisement for the teaching of Islam. It is not astonishing if people, seeing it, should turn away and think Islam to blame for their abasement. The point is, that Islam is not to blame for this, any more than ecclesiastical Christianity is to be praised for the present material progress of Christendom. Christianity had a priesthood and no freedom of thought. The centuries in which the Christian Church was supreme are now referred to as the dark ages. Islam had no priesthood, it had freedom of thought, and the ages when Islam prevailed in all its purity were ages of a singularly clear and brilliant light. It is their falling away from pure Islam which has brought ruin to the Muslims, their acceptance of something indistinguishable from a priesthood—or, in the words of the Quran, their "taking others for their lords besides Allah "—their pleasure in scholastic quibbles, their neglect of the advice to seek knowledge everywhere as a religious duty, their denial of free thought and their distrust of reason. At a certain period of their history, they began to turn their backs upon a part of what had been enjoined to them, they discarded half the Shari'ah—the part which ordered them to seek knowledge and education, and to study God's creation. And the Christians of the West about the same time, began to act according to that portion of the Shari'ah which the Muslims were discarding, and so advanced in spite of all the anathemas of their priesthood. The reason why it was ordained that there should be no priesthood in Islam is because ecclesiasticism is an enemy to human progress, and, therefore, opposed to true religion, of which the aim is shown in the Quran to be the progress and the liberation of humanity, not its stagnation and enslavement. Muslims all over the world are now awake to this ; they know that their humiliation is their own handiwork, and they see that they can only regain a noble status in the world by a return to Islam.

You may think that in this lecture I have wandered off from my appointed subject, which is culture, into the religious field. Islamic culture is so intricately bound up with religion, so imbued with the idea of Allah's universal sovereignty that I could not treat the subject properly without first giving you the indications I have given in this first address. In its grandeur and in its decadence, Islamic culture—whether we survey it in the field of science, or of art, or of literature, or of social welfare —has everywhere and always this religious inference, this all-pervading ideal of universal and complete theocracy. In all its various productions—some of them far from being what is usually called religious—this is evident. It is this which makes Islamic nationalism one with internationalism. For acceptance of the fact of Allah's universal sovereignty entails acceptance of the complementary fact of universal human brotherhood.

SECOND LECTURE.

Causes of Rise and Decline.

The particular cultural aspect of Islam of which I have to speak to-day is its humanity. By which I mean not only its goodwill and beneficence towards all men, but also, and especially its world-wide outlook. There is not one standard and one law for the Muslim and another for the outsider. In the Kingdom of Allah there are no favourites. The Sacred Law is one for all, and non-Muslims who conform to it are more fortunate than professed Muslims who neglect or disobey its precepts.

ان الله لا يغير ما بقوم حتي يغيروا ما با نفسهم .

> " Lo ! Allah changeth not the condition of a
> people, until they have changed that which con-
> cerneth themselves" that is, their conduct.

The test, as I have said before, is not profession of a creed, but conduct. All men are judged by conduct both in this world and the next.

I suppose you have all of you in mind at least an outline of the course of Muslim History. It may be divided into three periods—named after the three great nations and languages of the Muslim World—the Arab, the Persian and the Turkish. And I suppose every one of you has heard it said that Islam in early days was propagated by the sword.

The Holy Quran says :—

لا اكراه في الدين قد تبين الرشد من الغي فمن يـكفر
بالطاغوت ويومن بالله فقد استمسك بالعروة الوثقـي
لاانفصام لها والله سميع عليـم ·

" Let there be no compulsion in religion. The right
direction is henceforth distinct from error. And
he who rejecteth vain superstitions and believeth
in Allah hath grasped a firm handle which will
not give way. Allah is All-seeing, All-knowing.''

And again :—

وقاتلوا في سبيل الله الذين يقـاتلونـكم ولا تعتـدوا
ان الله لايحب المعتـدين ·

" Fight in the cause of Allah against those who fight
against you, but begin not hostilities. Verily
Allah loveth not aggressors.''

There are many other texts that I could quote to
prove that Muslims are forbidden to use violence towards
anyone on account of his opinions, and I can find not a
single text to prove the contrary. Whatever may have
happened later on in Muslim history, such injunctions
were not likely to be disobeyed in days when the Quran
was the only Law—a law obeyed alike by great and small
with passionate devotion, as the word of God.

The wars of Islam in the Holy Prophet's lifetime and
in the lifetime of his immediate successors were all begun
in self-defence, and were waged with a humanity and
consideration for the enemy never known on earth before.

It was not the warlike prowess of the early Muslims which enabled them to conquer half the then known world, and convert half that world so firmly that the conversion stands unshaken to this day. It was their righteousness and their humanity, their manifest superiority in these respects to other men.

You have to picture the condition of the surrounding nations, the Egyptians, the Syrians, the Mesopotamians and the Persians—ninety per cent. slaves. And they had always been in that condition. The coming of Christianity to some countries had not improved their status. It was the religion of the rulers and imposed upon the rank and file. Their bodies were still enslaved by the nobles, and their minds still enslaved by the priests. Only the ideal of Christianity, so much of it as leaked through to them, had made the common people dream of freedom in another life. There was luxury among the nobles, and plenty of that kind of culture which is symptomatic not of progress but corruption and decay. The condition of the multitute was pitiable. The tidings of our Prophet's embassies to all the neighbouring rulers, inviting them to give up superstitions, abolish priesthood and agree to serve Allah only, and the evil treatment given to his envoys, must have made some noise in all those countries; still more the warlike preparations which were being made for the destruction of the new religion. The multitude were no doubt warned that Islam was something devilish and that Muslims would destroy them. And then the Muslims swept into the land as conquerors, and by their conduct won the hearts of all those peoples.

2-A

In the whole history of the world till then, the conquered had been absolutely at the mercy of the conqueror, no matter how complete his submission might be, no matter though he might be of the same religion as the conqueror. That is still the theory of war outside Islam. But it is not the Islamic theory. According to the Muslim Laws of War, those of the conquered people who embraced Islam became the equals of the conquerors in all respects. And those who chose to keep their old religion had to pay a tribute for the cost of their defence, but after that enjoyed full liberty of conscience and were secured and protected in their occupations.

An utterly false interpretation has been given to the alternatives " Islam or the Sword " as if the sword meant execution or massacre. The sword meant warfare, and the alternatives really were : Islam (Surrender, in the spiritual sense), Islam (surrender, in the ordinary sense) or continued warfare. The people who did not surrender, were not fully conquered, and were still at war.

The Muslims intermarried freely with the conquered peoples of Egypt, Syria, Mesopotamia, Persia and all North Africa—a thing none of their conquerors (and they had known many in the course of history) had ever done before. The advent of Islam brought them not only political freedom but also intellectual freedom, since it dispelled the blighting shadow of the priest from human thought. The people of all those countries except Persia now claim Arabic as their native language and, if questioned as to their nationality, would say : We are sons of the Arabs. They all still regard the empire of Islam as the Kingdom of God on earth.

The result was what might be expected from so great a liberation of peoples who had never really had a chance before :—a wonderful flowering of civilisation which in the after generations bore its fruit in works of science, art and literature. In spite of its incessant wars, this is the most joyous period in history. In judging of it you must not take literally every word that you may read in European writers. You must make allowance for enemy propaganda then as now.

In my youth I saw a good deal of the Christian population of Syria, the descendants of such of the conquered people of those days as would not embrace Islam : and they used to speak of the early Muslim period almost as a golden age and of the Khalifa Umar ibn-ul-Khattáb almost as a benefactor of their religion. Folklore is sometimes more enlightening than written history. Yet even from written history, with a little research, you will discover that fanaticism towards Christians is hardly found in orthodox Islam till after the Crusades, though the Christians were not always easy subjects for toleration. Many of them thought it a religious virtue to insult the religion of Islam in public, and so court martyrdom from the natural indignation of the rulers. There were epidemics of this kind of religious mania at various times in different countries, and the sensible, calm manner in which the Muslim rulers dealt with them is one of the great things in Muslim history. I shall have to speak to you at length upon the subject of religious tolerance, so at present I will only read you an extract from Whishaw's " Arabic Spain." It runs :—" The epidemic of religious hysteria

which occurred at Cordova in the middle of the ninth
century is no doubt the reason why we have more informa-
tion about the state of the Church at that date than at
any other time during the Muslim rule. The Christians
were forbidden to enter the mosques or to vilify the
Prophet, under pain of conversion to Islam or death.
"This," says Florez (a Spanish writer), "was the most
criminal offence of the martyrs at that time, so that,
although they exalted the faith, the judges remained un-
moved until they heard them speak evil of Muhammad or
of his sect." According to the *Cronica general* two
"Martyrs" of the time, Rogelio and Serviodes, entered
the great Mosque of Cordova and began not only "preaching the faith," but also "the falseness of Muhammad and
the certainty of the hell to which he was guiding his followers." It is not surprising to learn that this performance
cost them their lives. Both the Muslim rulers and the
more sensible of the Christians did their best to prevent
these fanatics from throwing away their lives, and Reca-
fred, Bishop of Seville about 851 to 862, was distinguished
by his common sense in this matter. He forbade Christians to seek martyrdom when their rulers did not attempt
to make them deny their faith, and imprisoned "even
priests" who disobeyed him. Abdur Rahman II appointed him metropolitan of Andalucia that he might do the
same at Cordova, and there he imprisoned a number of
Christians, including St. Eulogius and the Bishop of
Cordova, doubtless to keep them out of mischief."

Similar outbursts of religious hysteria are recorded
in Eastern countries, which the Muslims bore with even

greater fortitude. The Christians as a rule were treated with the utmost toleration both in East and West.

Mr. G. K. Nariman, the well-known Parsi Orientalist, has proved from his research that the story of the wholesale massacre and expulsion of the Zoroastrians from Persia by the Arab conquerors is without historical foundation. There are Zoroastrians in Persia till the present day. In Syria the Christians used to speak of the times of the first four Khalifas, and of the Omayyad dynasty as the golden age of Muslim magnanimity ; which struck me then as curious because the Omayyads are generally given a bad name, on account of the personal character of some Khalifas of that house, but especially of the cruel tragedies which marked its rise to power. But it is a fact that Islam owes much to Bani Umayya historically. They preserved the simple, rational character of Islam—its Arab character ; they maintained in Damascus the intimate relations between the ruler and the subject which had characterised the Khilafat of Medina. In their days the Khalifa himself still climbed the pulpit and preached the Friday Khutba in the mosque. The anxieties of an exceptionally intelligent Khalifa of this house are depicted in a little anecdote in Kitab-ul-Fakhri.

قيل لعبد الملك لقد أسرع اليك الشيب قال شيبني صعود المنابر والخوف من اللحن وكان اللحن عندهم في غاية القبح .

"Someone said to Abdul Malik : Grey hairs have come to you very early. He answered : What has turned me grey is climbing pulpits with the fear of making a false quantity in Arabic. For to make a mistake in Arabic was with them a thing most horrible." They kept back the fanatical, "ecclesiastic" faction which even in those early days began to raise its head, and allowed time for the formation of a body of opinion which withstood the creeping paralysis of ecclesiasticism or scholasticism, and thus upheld the banner of Islam, for centuries. Next to the Khulafa-er-Rashidin, as a Khalifa of true Muslim character, comes Umar ibn Abdul Aziz of the Umayyads. And a scion of their house who fled westward after their downfall and massacre, founded a dynasty which made of Spain for many generations the most progressive and enlightened country in the West.

It is important for the student of history to remember that the Khilafat of Bani l-Abbâs represented a compromise between the out-and-out Sunnism of the Umayyads and the out-and-out Shi'ism of the Fatemites. For the Umayyads, the Abbâsids themselves were Shi'a. When in the Spanish Muslim Chronicles you read of Shi'as, they are not those whom we call Shi'a, but the people whom we regard as Sunnis, the followers of Bani'l–Abbâs, opponents of Bani Umayya; and it is important also to remember that the Khilafat of Bani'l–Abbâs represents a betrayal—nay, a double betrayal. On the one hand they had persuaded Ahl-ul-Beyt (*i.e.*, our Prophet's family) that they would set one of them upon the throne of the Khilafat; and on the other they had persuaded many earnest Sunnis, who till then had been supporters of Bani Umayya but objected to the dynastic Khilafat, that they would restore the original custom of electing the Khalifa from among the Muslims most distinguished for their public service. They did neither. They set up their own dynasty, they massacred the whole house of Bani Umayya, except one member who fled to Spain, because that house had made itself beloved in Syria, Najd, Egypt and throughout North Africa, and any member of it left alive would have been a formidable rival; and they persecuted Ahl-ul-Beyt on account of their standing claim to the Khilafat. It is a mistake to impute a religious character to the strife between those factions. It was a tribal quarrel of North Arabia against South Arabia, dating from pre-Islamic times.

T e simple, rational, Arab character of Muslim Government passed with the last of the Umayyads to Spain ; the Khilafat of the East was transferred to Bani 'l-Abbâs, who were already under Persian influence, and the capital was removed from Syria to Mesopotamia. The city of Baghdad—a much more glorious Baghdad than the present city of that name—a triumph of town-planning, sanitation, police ar angement and street-lighting. sprang into existence. There, and throughout the Empire in the next three centuries, Islamic culture reached its apogee. But except in Spain it had less and less of Arab simplicity and more and more of Persian magnificence. In the words of Mr. Guy Le Strange : at that period of the world's history, Cordova, Cairo, Baghdad and Damascus were the only cities in the world which had police regulations and street lamps. A reverence and a manner of address which the rightly guided Khalifas and the Umayyads would have repelled as blasphemous were accepted first, and then expected, by the Khalifas of the house of Abbâs.

The strict zenana system was introduced, and woman in the upper class of society, instead of playing the frank and noble part which she had played among the earlier Muslims, became a tricksy and intriguing captive. There was a tendency to narrow down Islam to the dimensions of a sect, which the rational Muslims were able to restrain only by the weight of their superior learning. The Khalifa leaned towards that tendency, because it flattered him, exalting his position high above its proper Muslim status.

The people, in a long period of uninterrupted prosperity, became unwarlike. There were little wars within the Empire now and then, but they did not affect the mass of the people for reasons which I shall explain when I address you on the laws of war. Many were the rational students of the Quran who pointed out the danger of this state of things, but the fanatical " ecclesiastic " faction flattered the Khalifa to a false security, declaring that he was especially favoured and protected by Allah, and that the glory of his realm would last for ever.

The defence of the frontiers was confided to the fighting tribes, chiefly to the Turks, who also formed the bodyguard of the Khalifa. These people, from the guardians, soon became the masters, of the nominal rulers. They were men of simple, downright, brutal character, of energy and commonsense, who did not hide their contempt for the luxurious and feeble princes who succeeded one another on the throne of the great Mamûn and Harûn-ar-Rashîd. One after another, they murdered or put them away with every circumstance of ignominy, but they did infuse some manhood into the declining Empire, which would have perished but for them, and keep at least its central provinces together in good order. Over the outlying provinces the Khalifa's rule was now purely nominal. As chief of the Muslims he sanctioned the appointment of the local ruler—a ceremony which had religious value in the people's eyes—and that was all. Persia declared itself independent. Egypt was conquered by a family known in history as the Fatemites or Obeydites who were descended from the Holy Prophet, though the Sunnis of those days denied their claim and said they were descendants of a Jew of Kerbela. They set up a rival Khilafat, conquered Palestine and Syria twice, and Hejjaz on e.

Nominally the Abbâsid Khilafat of Baghdad lasted for full five hundred years, but for the last three hundred and fifty years of its nominal duration the real sovereign power had passed already to the Turks, and its political prestige was that of Turkish chiefs :—first of the Seljuks-Toghrul Beg and Alp Arslân and Malik Shah—then of the Zenghis : Imâd-ud-din and his son Nûr-ud-dîn, and then of the Ayûbis. Sñlah-ud-din (the Saladin of the Crusading period), Malik Aâdil, Malik Kâmil and the rest. There was change of rulers. but the civilisation remained that of the Abbâsids. Indeed it hardly if at all deteriorated, and the condition of the common people throughout the Muslim Empire remained superior to that of any other people in the world in education, sanitation, public security and general liberty.

Its material prosperity was the envy of the Western world, whose merchant corporations vied with one another for the privilege of trading with it. What that prosperity must have been in its prime one can guess from the casual remark of a modern English writer with no brief for Muslims, with regard to Christian Spain : " Notwithstanding the prosperity which resulted from her privileged trade with the New World in the sixteenth century, her manufactures, and with them her real prosperity, began to decline under the Catholic kings, and continued to do so in fact, if not in appearance, until the expulsion of the Moriscoes,"— i.e., the last remaining Muslims—" by Philip III, completed the destruction begun by Isabel in the supposed interests of religion."

In other countries, even in Europe, in the same period, the peasantry were serfs bound to the land they cultivated, the artisans had still a servile status, and the mercantile communities were only just beginning, by dint of cringing and of bribery, to gain certain privileges. In the Muslim realm the merchant and the peasant and the artisan were all free men. It is true that there were slaves, but the slaves were the most fortunate of the people.

For the Holy Prophet's command to " clothe them with the cloth ye yourselves wear and feed them with the food which ye yourselves eat, for the slaves who say their prayers are your brothers " was literally obeyed, and so was the divine command to liberate them on occasions of thanks-giving, and as a penalty for certain breaches of the Sacred Law ; so that slavery would early have become extinct but for the spoils of war, and there was no such thing as a condition of perpetual or hereditary servitude. The slave was regarded as a son or daughter of the house, and in default of heirs inherited the property. In the

same way the slaves of kings have often in Islam inherited
the kingdom. It was no unusual thing for a man who
had no male descendant to marry his daughter to his slave
who took his name and carried on the honour of his house.
The devotion of the slaves to their owners and the favour
which the master showed the slaves became proverbial.
And when in after days the supply of slaves by warfare
ceased, and purchase was restricted in some regions,
like the Caucasus, where it had been customary, many
Muslims complained that kindness to slaves and emancipation of slaves was a duty enjoined upon them in the Quran,
and how could they perform that duty if no slaves
existed? That, of course, was a complete misapprehension.
misapprehension of the purpose of Islam, which was to
abolish slavery without a rough upheaval of society. But
that is an argument which I myself have actually heard
adduced to justify the cruel slave-trade with the Sudan.
The slave-trade was a horror which had no Islamic sanction. I do not say that there were no abuses in the Muslim
world, but I do say that they were not what Europeans
have imagined, and had no analogy with things similarly
named in Christendom ; just as the slavery which existed
in the Muslim world had no analogy with that of the
American plantations.

No colour or race prejudice existed in Islam. Black,
brown, white and yellow people mingled in its marts and
mosques and palaces upon a footing of complete equality
and friendliness. Some of the greatest rulers, saints and
sages in Islam have been men as black as coal like Jayyash
the saintly king of Yaman in the period of the Abbásid

decline, and Ahmad Al-Jabarti, the great historian of Egypt in the time of Arnaut Mohammad Ali, founder of the Khedivial dynasty. And if anyone thinks that there were no white people in that mighty brotherhood, be it known that there are no men whiter than the blond Circassians and the mountain folk of Anatolia who very early found a place in the Islamic confraternity. It was a civilisation in which there were differences of rank and wealth, but these did not correspond to class distinctions as understood in the West, much less to Indian caste distinctions.

A notable feature of this civilisation was its cleanliness at a time when Europe coupled filth with sanctity. In every town there was the hammâm, public hot baths, and public fountains for drinking and washing purposes. A supply of pure water was the first consideration wherever there were Muslims. And frequent washing became so much associated with their religion that in Andalusia in 1566 the use of baths was forbidden under severe penalties, because it tended to remind the people of Islam, and an unfortunate gardener of Seville was actually tortured for the crime of having washed while at his work. I myself in Anatolia have heard one Greek Christian say of another : " The fellow is half a Muslim ; he washes his feet."

The public food and water supplies were under strict inspection in all Muslim cities; and meat and other damageable food exposed for sale had to be covered with muslin as a protection from the dust and flies.

Intercourse was free between all classes of society, so was intermarriage, and everybody talked to everybody.

I am speaking now of something I have seen and known, for that civilisation still existed in essentials when I first went to Egypt, Syria and Anatolia. When I read (the Arabian Nights) Alf Leylah wa Leylah—most of the stories in which are of the period of the Abbâsid Khilafat though they were collected and published in Cairo some centuries later—I see the daily life of Damascus, Jerusalem, Aleppo, Cairo, and the other cities as I found it in the early nineties of last century. But when I saw it, it was manifestly in decay. What struck me even in its decay and poverty was the joyousness of that life compared with anything that I had seen in Europe. These people seemed quite independent of our cares of life, our anxious clutching after wealth, our fear of death.

And then their charity ! No man in the cities of the Muslim Empire ever died of hunger or exposure at his neighbour's gate.

They undoubtedly had something which was lacking in the life of Western Europe, while they as obviously lacked much which Europeans have and hold. It was only afterwards that I learnt that they had once possessed the material prosperity which Europe now can boast, in addition to that inward happiness which I so envied. It was only long afterwards, after twenty years of study, that I came to realise that they had lost material prosperity through neglecting half the Shari'ah, and that anyone can find that inward happiness who will obey the other half of the Shari'ah which they still observed.

Now let me go on with my story and tell you how the Muslim civilisation came to decay.

We have seen how it survived the decadence of the Abbâsid Khilâfat, upheld by the strong arms of Turkish slaves; for such was their position when they entered the Khalifa's service, though their chiefs soon gained the title of Amîr-ul-Umara and later of Sultân and Malik. You may wonder how it happened that, for centuries, the civilisation of Islam was altogether unaffected by this transfer of power from a cultured race to a race of comparative barbarians—nay, continued to progress in spite of it. The comparative barbarians were ardent Muslims. If they treated the Khalifa's person often with a brutal disrespect, born of intense contempt for such a worthless creature, it was not as the Khalifa that they so illtreated him but as a wretched sinner quite unfit to bear the title of Khalifa of the Muslims.

As a contemporary couplet, quoted by Ibn Khaldûn in his first Muqaddamah, puts it :—

خليفـة في قفص بين وصيف وبغي يـقـول ماقالا لـه
كما تقول الببغاء •

" A Khalifa in a cage, between a boy slave and a
   harlot.

" Repeating all they tell him parrotwise."

But the Khalifa was not the Khilafat. Though the Khalifa might be worthless, the Khilafat as an institution was still redoubtable, and commanded the respect of every Muslim, particularly of the simple minded Turkish soldiers. The civilisation of the Muslims had another guardian whom the Turkish warders treated with most grave respect. This was the opinion of the 'Ulama, the learned men,

expressed in the convocations of half a hundred universities, of which the delegates met together when required
in council. You must not think of them as what we now
call " 'Ulama ", by courtesy. The proper Arabic term for
the latter is fuquaha, and it had hardly come into general
use in those days when the science which we now know
as *fiqh* was still in its infancy.

The Muslim Universities of those days led the world
in learning and research. All knowledge was their field,
and they took in and gave out the utmost knowledge
attainable in those days. The Universities of those days
were, of course, different from those of modern times, but
they were then the most enlightened institutions in the
world. They were probably the most enlightened institutions that have ever been a part of a religion.

The German Professor Joseph Hell, in a little book on
the Arab civilisation which has lately been translated into
English by Mr. S. Khuda Bukhsh, thus writes of them :

" Even at the Universities religion retained its pri-
macy, for was it not religion which first opened the path
to learning ? The Quran, Tradition, Jurisprudence, there-
for—all these preserved their pre-eminence there. But it is
to the credit of Islam that it neither slighted nor ignored
other branches of learning ; nay, it offered the very same
home to them as it did to theology—a place in the mosque.
Until the 5th century of the Hijrah the mosque was the
university of Islam ; and to this fact is due the most
characteristic feature of Islamic culture " perfect freedom
to teach." The teacher had to pass no examination,
required no diploma, no formality, to launch out in that

capacity. What he needed was competence, efficiency, mastery of his subject. "

The writer goes on to show how the audience, which included learned men as well as students, were the judges of the teacher's competence and how a man who did not know his subject or could not support his thesis with convincing arguments could not survive their criticism for an hour, but was at once discredited.

These teachers of the Arab Universities were the foremost men of learning of their age ; they were the teachers of Modern Europe. It was one of them, a famous chemist, who wrote : " Hearsay and mere assertion have no authority in Chemistry. It may be taken as an absolutely rigorous principle that any proposition which is not supported by proofs is nothing more than an assertion which may be true or false. It is only when a man brings proof of his assertion that we say : Your proposition is true."

These 'Ulama were no blind guides, no mere fanatics. The Professors of those Universities were the most enlightened thinkers of their time. In strict accordance with the Prophet's teaching, it was they who watched over the welfare of the people and pointed out to the Khalifah anything that was being done against the rights of man as guaranteed by the Quran. It was they, indeed, who kept down the fanatic element, discouraged persecution for religious opinion, and saved Islamic culture from deteriorating in a thousand ways. They even forced ambitious Muslim rulers, in their un-Islamic strife, to refrain from calling on the people to assist them, to fight only with the help of their own purchased slaves and to respect all crops and cattle and non-combatants. They we:e able, by the enormous weight of their opinion with the multitude, to punish even rulers who transgressed the Sacred Law, in a way which brought them quickly to repentance ; and they exacted compensation for transgression.

The hosts of Chenghiz Khan, in their terrific inroad, destroyed the most important universities and masacred the learned men. This happened at a time when the Eastern boundaries of the Empire were but lightly guarded, the forces of the Turkish rulers having been drawn westward by the constant menace of the Crusades. Once the frontiers were passed, there was practically no one to oppose such powerful invaders. Then it was seen that another command, which is implicit in the Sharî'ah, had been forgotten or neglected : that every Muslim must have Military training. So strongly was that point impressed upon the public mind that it became the chief point of the Sharî'ah in public opinion thenceforward till the remnant of the Muslim Empire was partitioned by the powers of Europe only the other day.

The Muslim Empire revived after the attack of Chenghiz Khan and even made fresh progress--a progress so remarkable that it once more threatened Europe as a whole, and so aroused the old crusading animosity in modern dress, which was the secondary reason of its downfall. I say the secondary reason ; for the primary reason of the downfall must be sought in the Shari'ah, among those natural laws which always must control the rise and fall of nations.

3 A

The Empire was apparently progressing but it was progressing on the wave of a bygone impulse. The 'Ulama who sought for knowledge " even though it were in China" were no more. In their place stood men bearing the same high name of Ulama claiming the same reverence, but who sought knowledge only in a limited area, the area of Islam as they conceived it -not the world-wide, liberating and light-giving religion of the Quran and the Prophet, but an Islam as narrow and hidebound as religion always will become when it admits the shadow of a man between man's mind and God.

Islam, the religion of free thought, the religion which once seemed to have banished priestly superstition, and enslavement of men's minds to other men, for ever from the lands to which it came, had become—God forgive us ! —priest-ridden.

The pursuit of natural science had already been abandoned. All knowledge coming from without was reckoned impious, for was it not the knowledge of mere infidels ? Whereas the practice of the early Muslims was to seek knowledge even unto China, even though it were the knowledge of a heathen race. A growth of pride accompanied the cult of ignorance.

The Christian nations, which had been moved to the pursuit of science by the example of the Muslims had advanced materially just as the Muslims had advanced materially so long as they obeyed that portion of the Shari'ah or Sacred Law which proclaims freedom of thought and exhorts to the pursuit of knowledge and the study of God's creation. The Christian nations threw off the narrow shackles of ecclesiasticism and espoused free thought, and their advance in the material field was as surprising in its way as were the conquests of the early Muslims in their way.

But before I come to my conclusion, I must mention one great assertion of the universal nature of Islam which occurred in the darkest hour that Muslims ever knew. You will find it narrated in the first chapter of Kitâb-ul-Fakhri, where the author speaks of the importance of justice as a quality of the ruler according to the teaching of Islam, that when Sultan Hulaqu had taken Baghdad and held the unfortunate but worthless person of the Abbâsid Khalifa at his mercy, he put a question to the 'Ulama who had assembled at his bidding at the Mustan-siriyah—a question calling for a fatwa of the Learned, a question upon the answer to which depended the fate of the Khilafat : " Which is preferable (according to the Shari'ah) the disbelieving ruler who is just or the Muslim ruler who is unjust ?".

أيما افضل السلطان الكافر العادل او السلطان المسلم الجائر.

The 'Ulama were sitting all aghast, at a loss what to write, when Rizauddin Ali 'ibn Tawas, the greatest and most respected Aâlim of his time, arose and took the question paper and signed his name to the answer :

السلطان الكافر العادل.

" The disbelieving ruler who is just." All the others signed the answer after him. All knew that it was the right answer, for the Muslims cannot keep two standards, one for the professed believer and the other for the disbeliever, when Allah, as His messenger proclaimed, maintains one standard only. His standard and His Judgment are the same for all. He has no favourites. The favoured of Allah are those, whoever and wherever they may be, who keep His Laws. The test is not the profession of a particular creed, nor the observance of a particular set of ceremonies ; it is nothing that can be said or performed by anybody as a charm, excusing his or her shortcomings. The test is Conduct. The result of good conduct is good, and the result of evil conduct is evil, for the nation as for the individual. That is the teaching of Islam, and never has its virtue been more plainly illustrated than in the history of the rise and decline of Muslim civilisation.

The last Abbâsid Khalifa and his family were put to death most horribly, and for a little while the Mughal conquerors established their dominion over Western Asia. But in less than a generation, troubles in Persia called away the Mughals ; the Turkish chiefs revived their principalities which the Sultan of Qonia tried in vain to bring back to their old dependency. It was then that the Osmanli Turks first came upon the scene.

The rise of the Osmanli Turks, which brought the restoration of the Muslim Empire on a larger scale than ever, has interesting analogies with the history of the House of Timur—another Turki dynasty. The Ottoman Empire, at its zenith was not less glorious than that of Akbar, Shahjehan and Aurangzeb. It was then that the third great Muslim language blossomed in a literature which is utterly Islamic and yet definitely Turkish, covering all fields except the modern-scientific, an exquisite literature in an exquisite but very difficult language, which latter point—the language difficulty is perhaps the reason why the Orientalists of to-day, as a rule, ignore it. It was then that gems of architecture, mosques and palaces, arose. It was then that all the remnant of Islamic learning flocked to Brûsa, Adrianople and at last Stambûl, the successive capitals of the Osmanli Sultans, who were munificent patrons of every kind of literary and artistic merit, themselves generally poets of distinction.

The poetry of the Ottoman Turks is, to me, strangely appealing : it is usually sad, as is but natural to a race of men who, when they thought a little deeply, had always to reflect that death was near to them ; but it is never despondent, and the passionate—almost desperate—love of nature it displays is really sincere, a characteristic of the people. The most characteristic productions of Turkish literature have an affinity with what I have read,—though in translations only—of Chinese literature. But it is their beautiful home life to which I should point if asked to indicate the greatest contribution of the Turks to Muslim culture ; it has—or had, for I am speaking of before the war—in common with their poetry, the nobility and depth which everything acquires for those who are prepared to die at any minute for a cause which they regard as worthy ; and the way they went to death and the way their women bore it—the dignity, the grace of every action of their daily lives. Those are achievements every nation in the world might envy.

The Osmanli Turks were soldiers first, poets second, politicians third, and theologians fourth. It was not their fault if they took the word of others in the matter of religion. The language of religion was Arabic, and only learned men among them knew Arabic, though all were taught to recite the Quran, " for a blessing " : that is, without thought or understanding of the meaning, as a sort of charm. They were soldierly in all they did, and they trusted their spiritual experts as they trusted their military experts. The people were contented in the decline as they had been in the prime of the civilisation, for the decline came gradually, imperceptibly, and affected all alike ; nor were they conscious of the deterioration which had actually taken place, since all the accustomed paraphernalia still existed, with a shadow of the former pomp.

The schools, primary and secondary, still existed ; so did the universities, but they were now engaged in teaching, the former the Quran without the meaning, the latter all the hair-splitting niceties of Fiqh—religious jurisprudence—a science of great use to every Muslim, but taught in such a way as to imprison the intelligence. The machinery of justice, sanitation, police and public works still existed, only it had ceased to function properly. It was not until some Powers of Europe began to interfere in order to improve the status of the Christian subjects of the Porte that the Turks became aware that they had dropped below the standard of the times. It was only after they had met a modern army in the field that they realised that their whole military system and equipment was now antiquated ; and then, to do them justice, the Turks tried with all their might to recover the lost ground.

If they were the leaders, all unconscious, in the decadence of Islam, they became afterwards the conscious leaders in the struggle for revival. The Turkish literature of the last fifty years is altogether different from the older Turkish literature. From the poetic works of Nâmiq Kamâl and Ekrem, full of patriotic ardour, to the remarkable work of the late prince Saïd Halîm Pasha entitled " Islamlash'maq " (Islamise) in which the principles of the Sharî'ah are expounded in modern terms and shown to be somewhat different from those taught by its alleged exponents, and leading to quite different consequences, the modern Turkish literature i. all progressive and constructive. It is full of hope in spite of the terrific ordeals the Turkish nation and the Muslim Empire had to undergo. Alghâzilar, the warriors of Islam, are still the heroes, and ‏نازلي كفن‏ ." the bloody shroud " is still the guerdon of the bravest of the brave ; but the Jihâd which is celebrated is no longer in defence of a dying empire, it is the true Jihâd of Islam, the Jihâd of human freedom, human progress, human brotherhood, in allegiance to Allah.

The Turkish revolution was the small beginning of a great revival of Islam, of which the signs can now be seen in every quarter of the Muslim world. Everyone now sees that ecclesiasticism—or scholasticism, if you prefer the word ; it is more accurate—was the cause of the decline, and that Islam, as planted in the world, requires all available light and knowledge for its sustenance. The Muslims must seek knowledge even though it be in China. Islam can never thrive in darkness and in ignorance.

THIRD LECTURE.

Brotherhood.

I have to talk to you to-day about Islamic brother-hood as an ideal and an institution. To begin with, I will quote but one passage, out of a hundred which I could quote in this connection, from the Holy Quran:—

يا ايها الذين آمنوا اتـقـوا الله حق تقـاتـه ولا تموتـن الا وانتم مسلمون – واعتصموا بـحبل الله جميعاً ولا تفرقوا واذكروا نـعـمـة الله عليكم اذ كنتم اعـدآء فالـف بين قلوبكم فاصبحتم بنعمتـه اخـواناً وكنتـم علي شـفا حفرة من النار فانقذكم منها كذا لـك يـبين الله لكم آ ياتـه لعلـكم تـهتـد ون .

> "O ye who believe! Observe your duty to Allah with right observance, and die not till ye have surrendered (unto him).

> "And hold fast, all of you together, to the cable of Allah, and do not separate. And remember Allah's favour unto you: how ye were enemies and He made friendship between your hearts so that ye became as brothers by His grace and (how) ye were on the brink of an abyss of fire, and He did save you from it. Thus Allah maketh clear His revelations unto you in order that ye may be guided."

These two verses of the Holy Quran are a reminder of the progress already made in a few months owing to

the advent of Islam, and a command to all the Muslims
to continue in the way of progress by clinging to the cable
of Allah, the Sacred Law, and never again to return to the
unhallowed state of warring tribes and hostile classes
which had reached such a pitch as to threaten human
culture in Arabia with complete destruction. Our Prophet
(may God bless and keep him) said: The Muslims
are as a wall, one part supporting another. The Muslims
are all one body. If the eye is injured the whole body
suffers, and if the foot is injured, the whole body suffers.

In his speech from Jebel 'Arafât to a great multitude
of men, who but a few months or years before had all been
conscienceless idolators, on the occasion of the Hajjat-al-
Wadâ', "the farewell pilgrimage," his last visit to Mecca,
he said:

> "O people, listen to my words with understanding
> for I know not whether, after this year, I shall
> ever be among you in this place:

> "Your lives and property are sacred and inviol-
> able one to another until you appear before your
> Lord, even as this day and this month are sacred
> for all, and remember you will have to appear
> before your Lord who will demand from you an
> account of all your acts.

> "The Lord hath prescribed to every man his share
> of inheritance; no testament to the prejudice of
> heirs is lawful.

> "The child belongeth to the parent, and the
> violator of wedlock shall be stoned.

4

" Whoever falsely claimeth another for his father
or his master, the curse of God and of the angels
and of all mankind shall be upon him.

" O people, ye have rights over your wives and
your wives have rights over you. It is their
duty not to break their wifely faith, nor commit
any act of manifest indecency. If they do so
ye have authority to confine them in separate
rooms and to punish them but not severely·
But if they refrain, clothe them and feed them
properly. Treat your women with loving kindness, for they are with you as prisoners and
captives. They have no power over anything that
concerneth them. Lo, ye have taken them on the
security of Allah and made their persons lawful
to you by the words of Allah.

" Be faithful to the trust imposed on you, and
shun transgression."

" Usury is forbidden, the debtor shall return
only the principal; and the beginning will
be made with the loans of my uncle Abbâs, son
of Abdul Mutallib.

" Henceforth the vengeance for blood practised in the
time of ignorance is forbidden, and the feud of
blood is abolished beginning with the murder
of my cousin Rabîa' ibn Harith ibn Abdul
Mutallib.

" And your slaves! See that ye feed them with
such food as ye yourselves eat, and clothe
them with the stuff ye yourselves wear ; and if

they commit a fault which ye are not ready to forgive, then part with them, for they are servants of your Lord, and must not be ill-treated. The slaves who say their prayers are your brothers.

"O people! Listen to my words and understand them. Know that all Muslims are brothers one to another; ye are one fraternity. No thing belonging to one of you is lawful to his brother unless given out of free goodwill. Guard yourselves from committing injustice.

"Let him that is present tell it to him who is absent. Haply he who shall be told will remember better than him who hath heard."

At the end of his discourse the Holy Prophet, moved by the sight of the devotion of that multitude, most of whom had been the enemies of Islam but a little while ago, exclaimed:—

"O Lord, I have delivered my message, and accomplished my work."

The hosts below made answer with one voice:
"Aye, that thou hast!"
He said:

"O Lord, I beseech Thee, be Thou witness to it!"

Had ever man such fulness of success? Was ever man more humble in his hour of triumph?

Notice how Muḥammad (God bless him!) never was content with precept. He always strengthened precept with example. Though he had become, in fact, the

Emperor of Arabia, he never sat upon a throne and issued edicts. He was always one among his people, his leadership being that of the Imam before the congregation, setting the example, foremost in obedience to the law which he himself proclaimed. When he proclaimed the brotherhood of Muslims he did not exempt himself. He was, and is, the elder brother of all Muslims. Of all he taught he is the great example.

Now this subject of human brotherhood is one upon which the Muslims have no apologies to make to any other creed or nation or community. Here they have a great achievement, as clearly visible to-day as when the Prophet spoke, to show for an example to the nations.

Other religious communities declare their belief in the Fatherhood of God and the brotherhood of man, but they have shown no practical result of that belief to help a struggling world; so little help has their ideal been that the struggling world, in its convulsive efforts to escape from misery, has turned its back upon religion as one of its oppressors, and sought help in other humanistic formulas, associated, through reliance on a false analogy, not with religion but with atheism or agnosticism—" Liberty, equality, fraternity "—the materialistic gospel of Karl Marx, and so forth.

" Liberty, equality, fraternity." Which is practicable? Liberty and equality in human society must always be only relative, for they are positively unattainable. The liberty of an individual or a nation must be bounded by the liberties of neighbouring individuals or nations, and opinions differ as to what constitutes liberty and equality.

To talk about the rights of man as something intrinsic, existing apart from man's position in society, is to talk nonsense, from our Muslim point of view. Man was not born with rights. He was born with instincts and gifts. He acquires rights only as he learns to curb and to control those instincts and to use those gifts for the common weal. His rights are in exact proportion to the duties he performs, and otherwise have no existence.

To claim equality for all men is absurd, and to seek to enforce it is to seek to paralyse humanity. To claim liberty for all men is to claim a thing concerning the nature and measure of which people hold widely divergent opinions, and will, moreover, fight for their opinions. One man's ideal of liberty is the British Constitution, and another's is the Soviet System.

In the strife about liberty and equality, fraternity is quite forgotten and grows more remote than ever. Yet fraternity is attainable wherever men of honest purpose and good-will agree together to obey a certain code of Laws religiously. Yet, to look at the past history and the present condition of the world, we might think it a Utopia, if it were not for the example of Islam. It is this that makes one inclined to propound the axiom that no real democracy in the shape of human brotherhood can exist anywhere apart from the ideal of Theocracy.

The Prophet of Nazareth brought an ideal of human brotherhood; which depends practically on the ideal of theocracy which prevailed among the Jews. Consequently, it was never put in practice since theocracy has never been the system of Government, much less the basis of society, in Christendom.

Our Prophet not only proclaimed the fact of universal human brotherhood, but for the first time in the history of the world, made of it a principle and fact of common law. All the ordinances of Islam tend towards it, and it is shown to be the only ground of genuine human progress. Social inequality remained; there remained those restrictions upon individual liberty which must exist in every organised society. But brotherly relations were established permanently between men and nations, however different in character and rank and wealth and power. "The slaves who say their prayers are your brothers." And it was no mere pious phrase. They were actually so treated. In the intercourse between nations also there was established a brotherhood which still endures. The spirit of aggressive nationality was abolished among Muslims by our Prophet's saying:

> "He is not of us who sides with his tribe in aggression, and he is not of us who calls others to help him in tyranny, and he is not of us who dies while assisting his tribe in injustice."

Islam became a super-nationality which extinguished nationalism in the body of Islam, and made the idea of a man's fighting for "his country right or *wrong*" appear a madness of the time of ignorance, as the period in Arabia before the coming of Muhammad (God bless him!) is called. He also said that an Ethiopian slave who does right is more worthy to be made the ruler than a Sharîf of Quraish who does wrong. Social service was acknowledged as the strongest claim to the respect and reverence of the community, a claim much stronger than the claim of birth or riches or brute force.

"Do unto others as you would that others should do unto you."

How can you bring that maxim home to stupid individuals and most individuals are made obtuse to social truth of this kind by self-interest except by making them feel when they do wrong to others exactly what those others felt when wrong was done to them. Hence the law of strict retaliation, which some people seem to think in some way cruel. It is not cruel, as enjoined on Muslims, who are forbidden to go beyond the measure of the criminal's own deed. They are forbidden to make an example in punishment—that is to punish a criminal more ruthlessly than his crime demands with the idea of deterring others or intimidating them.

اياكم والمثلة ولو بالكلب العقور.

"Woe to you if ye indulge in exemplary punishment even of a savage dog." Strict justice in retaliation is the only example in punishment which has genuine human value.

The laws of Allah as revealed in the Quran are simply that maxim: "Do unto others, etc." extended to collective as well as individual human conduct, codified and reasoned out in detail in such a way that the ignorant and the intelligent, the nation and the individual, alike can know for certain what their duty is in given circumstances. Usury is anti-social, is unbrotherly, because it is to take a mean advantage of a brother's need; wherefore it is written

يمحق الله الربوا ويربي الصدقات والله لا يحب كل كفار اثيم.

> "Allah maketh usury barren and alms-giving fruitful. Allah loveth not any impious and guilty (creature)."

To hoard up riches also is anti-human, therefore the Muslim is adjured to spend of the wealth which God has given him, all that is superfluous (العفو) *i.e.*, in excess of his own requirements. The verse which I just quoted concerning usury contains a truth which many people have lost sight of in these days. It is that the rush for riches does not increase the sum of human culture or human happiness, which can only be done by the equitable circulation and continual dispersal of wealth—that is to say by discouraging the greed of individuals, and encouraging their generosity.

Many, even among Muslims, today speak of the law against usury as antiquated. Such people cannot have looked on the pageant of the present day with seeing eyes. A good part of the business transactions of modern life, which the law of Islam forbids if strictly interpreted, seem harmless enough when compared with the more outrageous forms of usury which every decent human being would condemn. As a substitute for the worst usury, the present financial system seems desirable. But its general social influence, upon the whole, has been against fraternity. Why do socialism, communism, syndicalism today threaten the whole structure of the capitalist order of society—an order of society which has had a bare century of existence, and which its supporters are now hurrying to bolster up with tardy measures for the relief of suffering *majorities* ? Why was it that when Bolshevism came to power in Russia the first thing that it did was to abolish interest ? Why is it that the abolition of interest is included in every Socialist programme and Utopia ? It is because the capitalist form of society is founded upon usury, and that is held by the thinkers opposed to it to be the reason why it is productive of so much social evil and injustice.

Trade is licensed by the Sharî'ah, which strictly forbids usury. Here it is well to remember that the kind of trade licensed by the Quran was not the ruthless profiteering trade of modern times, much of which, in my opinion, must be classed as usury, in the Islamic sense, in so far as it takes unfair advantage of the crying needs of men and women. Drunkenness is anti-social ; gambling is anti-social. Therefore, the use of intoxicating liquor is forbidden, so are games of chance. Private property is sanctioned in Islam and strongly safeguarded; but the idea of property as belonging absolutely to the individual, to do exactly what he likes with it, and to leave it by bequest to whom he likes is anti-social, therefore, it is discountenanced. All property is a trust from God, and is held upon conditions clearly stated in the Sacred Law. A certain portion of the income must be paid out to the poor, a certain portion to the community every year. And when a man dies his property must be divided among certain relatives, women as well as men, in fixed proportions.

Aggressive nationalism is anti-human, therefore it was abolished, as already mentioned. Race and colour prejudices disappear completely in the Muslim brotherhood, and the differences of class are purged of arrogance or humiliation, and reduced to differences of occupation.

4-A

Islamic civilisation is a complete system, covering every field of human thought and action from the spiritual to the menial—a system which has been tried in practice with success.

I have traced the decline of Muslim civilisation in my previous lecture and have shown that its cause is to be found in the neglect of certain precepts of the Sacred Law. The system of civilisation is nowhere to be found completely operative to-day. But there is one respect in which the Muslim Community is as far ahead of the rest of the world as it was in the days of Umar (رضي الله عنه .) or the second Umar or Harûn-ar-Rashîd or Salâh-ud-dîn or Suleymân the Magnificent, and that is brotherhood.

Where, in the whole history of the world, will you find anything to compare with this great brotherhood of all sorts and conditions of human beings bound together by a tie so strong that the fierce assaults of hostile armies, the cunning efforts of diplomacy have failed to break it ? A brotherhood composed not of a single class or nation but of innumerable classes, many nations.

A League of Nations has been started to try to do a part of the work Islam has done, to bring the varying nations into unison and frame a code of international law conducive to peace and progress. But it is starting, at a disadvantage, for it admits the principles of aggressive nationalism and imperialism. It has to deal with nations which regard those anti-human principles as respectable and even noble. It is hard to see how, starting from such a point, so handicapped, it can ever reach the true solution of the problem, which is that nations have the same rights as individuals and that the same moral, laws and standards must be applied to them as are applied in the case of individuals. The Islamic brotherhood should be the model of the League of Nations, for here the peoples are at heart united. Shattered though the Muslim realm has been politically, the solidarity of the peoples remains unimpaired, unbroken. Some critics, seeing it hold firm against all pressure from without, exclaim : " The Muslims even when they pretend to be nationalists have no patriotism, only fanaticism." They would have us exchange our supernational outlook for the outlook of aggressive nationality. If Muslims did that they would indeed (in the words of the Quran) " barter that which is best for that which is lowest " as surely as did Bani Israîl of old. Islam is thirteen hundred years ahead of Europe in such matters.

There are certain ordinances, the observance of which tend to preserve and to extend this universal brotherhood of Islam; which is without comparison, for it has bound together black and white and brown and yellow people in complete agreement and equality, has reconciled the claims of rich and poor, the governor and the governed, slave and free. One of the most important of them is the daily and the weekly prayers in congregation, where all Muslims of every degree stand as equals in humanity, and the Imam, the leader, is chosen not for rank or wealth, but piety. Another is the yearly pilgrimage—a most important institution to the culture of Islam, which is often quoted by opponents as a proof that Islam is hopelessly behind the times—these pleasure-seeking times ! On the pilgrimage, kings, peasants, nobles, workmen, rich and poor, all wear the same coarse clothing, perform the same ceremonies in the same way, equal as all mankind are equal in the hour of death. Every Muslim who is able to do so, without injury to those dependent on him, has to make the pilgrimage at least once in his life, has to make his will, arrange his worldly business, forsake his home and occupation, and embark upon a long and tedious journey for no earthly gain. There are people in the world who think that useless. I do not.

Then there is the fast of Ramadhan, the yearly month of training, when every Muslim who is not sick or on a journey has to fast in the strictest sense of the word from dawn till after sunset. The king, the peasant—everybody. There are people in the world who think that senseless. I do not; nor will any one who takes the trouble to reflect a little on the rough vicissitudes of human life and on the kind of training men require to face them manfully. All men worthy of the name must prepare themselves to become soldiers on emergency. Most of all, those who stand for principles essential to the progress of humanity.

In reality, all these ordinances do but ring the changes on the Prophet's saying:—

موتوا قبل ان تموتوا‌   "Die before you die," the sacrifice of man's will to the will of God as revealed in the Quran and manifested in creation, which is Islam itself. In the daily prayers, the prayer-mat signifies the grave, the rakaa (bowing) means submission to the will of God as Sovereign of this world, and the Sujûd (prostration) is a figurative death, surrender to our Lord as Monarch of the Day of Judgment.

In Ramadhan, the Muslim changes his whole round of life, and rich and poor endure the pangs of hunger till, when sunset comes, the king gives heartfelt thanks to God for such a simple matter as a glass of water.

In the pilgrimage the Muslim goes as to his death, having settled all his worldly business, paid up all his debts, made his will and freed himself from earthly cares.

Life, with its pleasures and pursuits, divides mankind and makes men rivals, enemies. Death—the mighty leveller as it has been called—makes all men brothers. It is a perpetual warning, set before all of us, never to forget that all are brothers in the sight of God, and that our pride, ambition, wealth and power, all that here makes distinction between man and man, will fall from us when we reach that awful boundary. Death is, indeed, the most important fact of life, and a scheme of life which strove to ignore or belittle it would be misleading. At the same time, to spend one's life in contemplation of the fact of death would be to neglect the duties of this world, of which Allah is King as much as of the others. Islam presents us with a way of life, by following which men lose the fear of death and view it in its true perspective. And the way is joyous, anything but gloomy. These things are simple for the simple, and profound for men of intellect. For all, they are the firmest ground of human brotherhood.

Islam is, as I have said, in this matter of fraternity, as far ahead of the rest of the world today as it was in its days of splendour. By that I do not mean that there has been no falling off, but merely that nowhere else is to be found even the smallest attempt at such a human brotherhood. There has been falling off, and, as in every other case where Muslim culture has declined, it can be traced to the neglect of some provision of the Sharî'ah. In this case it is due to the neglect of Zakâh—the Muslim poor rate. The Arabic word Zakâh means growth by cultivation.

When Zakâh was regularly collected and distributed and any surplus put into the Beyt-ul-Mâl, a sort of bank which backed the efforts of the whole community, we read that there were no needy Muslims. In countries where it is still regularly collected and distributed—as, for instance, Najd—there are no needy Muslims. In countries where it is neglected they abound. This neglect, and the consequent misfortune of the Muslim brotherhood, is not the fault of the people. It is the fault of the despotic Governments of former days who took all such matters out of the people's control, and so in time deprived them of initiative, making them wait for Government officials to do things for them, even things which it was their Muslim right and duty to do for themselves. It should be the first care of every group of Muslims who seek progress to revive Zakâh and the Beyt-ul-Mâl with proper safeguards.

Indeed they would do well to study the whole Muslim system of finance. People seem to think that there was no such thing, that Muslims are by nature unbusinesslike, and that there was never a Muslim financier till English training gave us Mr. Hydari.

There were many great Muslim financiers, and the Muslim system of finance was a complete system. Only it is difficult for modern men of affairs even to begin to understand it, because its aim was not private profit or State profit, but public benefit, the welfare and progress of the whole Muslim brotherhood. It was a potent factor in the success of the Muslim civilisation, and the decline of that civilisation synchronised with the gradual neglect of it. Books have been written on it by Western Orientalists—notably a large volume by an American University Professor who treats it as a serious contribution to civilised thought. Being framed in strict accordance with the Sacred Law, that old Muslim system, which was practised with success in a huge Empire, is of special interest to those Muslims who find their conscience troubled by the present system of finance and commerce.

It is the surest, simplest, most effective way for building up a strong community or restoring a broken or decayed one; but it is a way requiring some degree of sacrifice from everyone. If we obey the Sharî'ah we have to spend what God has given us, not only money but all other gifts, in God's way, not our own way. The modern world says "Save all you can, bank it, invest it, place it out at interest." The Holy Quran says "Spend whatever remains over"—that is, after you have satisfied your needs and the needs of those dependent on you, have paid your poor rate, and bestowed a due amount in charity— and spend it in such a way as directly to benefit your fellow-men, to encourage the deserving, and increase the sense of human brotherhood. It absolutely forbids usury, which means deriving profit from a brother's need, as it forbids Isrâf, which means the squandering of money or of other gifts of God on things frivolous and vain, of no real use to anyone. Some of its injunctions seem amazing at the present day until one realises that they refer to a state of society founded not on the idea of competition but on that of brotherhood—a state of society in which no one is allowed to starve, a state of society which, so long as it existed in a flourishing condition, was the most successful that the world has ever known from the point of view of the greatest good of the greatest number. It seems to me essential that Muslims of today should study carefully the proper Muslim system of finance.

Another great cause of deterioration is neglect of the command that every Muslim, male and female, shall be educated; which neglect is nowhere so deplorably apparent as in India. In other Muslim countries—in the Turkish Empire and in Egypt, for example, a system of universal education did exist, and there were schools for everybody before the modern education came in vogue. It was an ancient system of education, which had once been in advance of the world-standard, but had become old and somnolent and purblind. But every Muslim did at least acquire a working knowledge of the teachings of Islam and his religious duties. In India there is not even that. There are people classed as Muslims here in India who only know the Kalima, if they know that; who are absolutely ignorant of all religion. Then, in every country, many were chary of admitting European knowledge and so fell behind, saw others placed above them for reasons which they could not understand, became disheartened and aggrieved—a fruitful source of poverty. All this can be remedied in time, and many are at work to remedy it. But while it is so it must dim for all onlookers the brightness of the great example of fraternity which Muslims do in truth set to the world.

Wars between Muslim potentates, differences of political opinions, divergences of race and colour do not affect this bond of brotherhood. That is something which outsiders always fail to understand. There is something in the words " I am a Muslim " and in the greeting " As-Salamu Aleykum " which touches the heart of every other Muslim. We differ not as outside people differ, radically. We differ not concerning ends, but only means. The end which every Muslim has in view is the end which Islam has in view, namely the building up of world-wide human brotherhood in allegiance to the One God. We differ only as to the way in which it is to be done; and the spread of proper Muslim education, allowing everybody to have access to the words of the Quran, and to compare their teaching with the requirements of the age in which we live, will very largely mitigate our differences, and remove misconceptions with regard to the scope of the Muslim brotherhood, which properly includes not only Muslims, technically so-called, but all who seek to establish the Kingdom of God on earth.

FOURTH LECTURE.

Science, Art and Letters.

This time I am going to speak to you of the achievements of the followers of Islam in Science, Literature and Art.

In this brief survey I shall, with your permission, leave out from our discussion the greatest achievement of all, the Holy Quran itself, because in the whole cultural development of Islam that must be taken for granted. It is not one of the achievements of Islamic culture; it is the inspiration and the cause of all achievements.

To take Science first: The frequent appeals to human reason and exaltation of the natural above the miraculous in the Quran, with such clear injunctions of the Holy Prophet as those I have already quoted:

> " To seek knowledge is a religious duty for every Muslim and every Muslimah."

> " Seek knowledge though it be in China " and most remarkable of all, his saying :

> " An hour's contemplation and study of God's creation is better than a year of adoration ",

started Muslim civilisation on a basis on free thought and free inquiry in the name of Allah.

To look for scientific treatises in the Quran, or indeed in any Scripture claiming to be the word of God, is futile. Divine revelation is only of laws which man is unable to find out for himself; the physical Laws of nature he can find out for himself by research and experiment, and it is part of man's development and growth to make that effort after knowledge. When the infinite intelligence speaks to the limited intelligence it must be in the language of the latter's limitations, or the message would seem nonsense to the little people, who would turn away.

There are passages in the Quran which might be taken as opposed to modern science by any one who read them separately, without the context : they are part of the intelligible language of the time ; the language of to-day would have been unintelligible. On the other hand there are many passages which seem to take us to the utmost heights of human knowledge.

I quote but three of them :—

وما من دابة في الارض ولا طائر يطير بجناحيه الا
أمم أمثالكم ما فرطنا في الكتاب من شيئ ثم إلي ربهم
يحشرون ·

> " And there is not an animal in the earth nor flying
> creature flying upon wings but is a people like
> unto yourselves. We have neglected nothing in
> the book of Our decrees. Then unto their Lord
> they will be gathered."

سبحان الذي خلق الازواج كلها مما تنبت الارض
ومن أنفسهم ومما لا يعلمون ·

> " Praise be to Him who created all the wedded
> pairs, of that which the earth groweth, and of
> their own kind, and of kinds which they know
> not."

The most recent of all scientific discoveries is that everything exists in pairs as male and female, even the rock crystals, even electricity.

And, to me, the most significant words of all, though quite beyond my fathoming, are these : " And ye shall not be judged save as a single soul." The soul of all mankind. Perhaps the soul of all created life !

The Quran undoubtedly gave a great impetus to learning, especially in the field of natural science ; and, if, as some modern writers have declared, the inductive method, to which all the practical modern discoveries are chiefly owing, can be traced to it, then it may be called the cause of modern scientific and material progress.

The Muslims set out on their search for learning in the name of God at a time when Christians were destroying all the learning of the ancients in the name of Christ. They had destroyed the Library at Alexandria, they had murdered many philosophers including the beautiful Hypatia. Learning was for them a devil's snare beloved of the pagans. They had no injunction to " seek knowledge even though it were in China." The manuscripts of Greek and Roman learning were publicly burnt by the priests. The Western Romans had succumbed to barbarism. The Eastern Roman Emperors kept their library and entertained some learned men ; but within their palace walls. The priests ruled everything beyond. We find the Khalifa Al-Mamun making war upon the Christian Emperor of Constantinople for the sole purpose of obtaining certain ancient books and the persons of certain men of learning versed in ancient sciences. These were shut up in the imperial palace at

Constantinople but when they came to Baghdad their learning became useful to humanity; for those learned men, in collaboration with the learned men among the Muslims, were set to work at once on the translation of the ancient books. Thus the Muslims saved the ancient learning from destruction and passed its treasures down to modern times.

In their Chemistry—which was of course three parts Alchemy—the Muslim scientists were constantly experimenting and, what is more, recorded and compared results. Before that time such scientific knowledge as existed in the East had been jealously kept secret by its owners for their personal repute as wonder-workers. The Muslim scientists published their results and welcomed the advice and help of other scientists. They did not jump to conclusions, but worked step by step on the inductive method, which they were the first to adopt, and they recorded all observed phenomena. The data which they thus obtained are the acknowledged basis of modern chemical science with its wonderful discoveries.

It was a Muslim chemist of the third Islamic century who wrote :—

" Hearsay and mere assertion have no authority in chemistry. It may be taken as an absolutely rigorous principle that any proposition which is not supported by proofs is nothing more than an assertion which may be true or false. It is only when a man brings proof of his assertion that we say : Your proposition is true."

That chemist was no exception among Muslim men of learning of the first eight or nine centuries. All were in search of proof, all were experimenting.

In Physics they worked in the same way, experimenting and recording the results of their experiments. They were mathematicians, and geometricians. They invented Algebra as we know it. They had a very complete science of Botany as any comprehensive Arabic, Persian or Turkish Dictionary will prove. But this is so completely lost at the present day by the majority that if you ask a fairly educated Arab the name of some wild plant he will, ten to one, reply : " It is a kind of grass " or with supreme contempt : " it is a wild plant." Only plants which have some homely use or some peculiar perfume are known by name to the majority to-day.

In Natural History, they began by following Aristotle—a blind guide to our modern thinking, but the best obtainable and generally respected in those days—but here also they observed for themselves, and noted down their observations, thus correcting Aristotle and advancing scientific knowledge.

In Geography they made a great advance. The Arabs were the greatest traders, travellers and navigators of that age, and they recorded everything of note they met with in their travels. That part of the earth's surface which the Arabs regularly visited was pretty accurately charted, and the political, social and commercial condition of the inhabitants, with fauna, flora, exports and imports, was generally known, being taught in the schools.

In Medicine, both theory and practice, their achievements were so notable that for centuries the Yunani system—that is, the Greek system translated into Arabic and enriched by the practical observations and experiments of the Arabs—was accepted throughout Europe no less than Asia. I may add that the Greek contribution to this most valuable science would have been lost but for the enterprise and learning of the Muslims.

The Muslim physicians were the first to inculcate the virtues of fresh air, and perfect cleanliness. They were the first to establish Hospitals in which the patients were grouped in separate wards according to their diseases, where cleanliness and fresh air formed part of the treatment, and in which the patient's comfort was the first consideration.

In a later age—so late as the eighteenth century—the Turks gave back to Europe the knowledge of the ancients as to the benefits to be derived from mineral springs and change of air and water; and it was from Turkey in the eighteenth century that the notion of inoculation was first brought to Europe. It was among the useful things brought back by Mr. Stuart Wortley Montagu, husband of the Lady Mary, whose " Letters " are of a nature to dispel false notions as to the relative barbarism of the Turks in those days.

Their Astronomy was, of course, three parts astrology, but they kept observatories fitted with instruments of some precision, and carefully recorded all their observations. The best known of these observatories are those of Spain and the particularly fine Observatory at Samarcand.

Astronomers compared notes with travellers, geographers and mathematicians; and it was as the result of their combined observations, that the revolving terrestrial globe happened to be part of the educational equipment of the Spanish Muslim Universities at the time when the learned Bruno was burnt at a slow fire by the inquisition for upholding the Copernican theory of the revolution of the earth, and before the even greater Galileo was forced by persecution to recant and sign a solemn declaration that the earth was fixed immovably as the Bible said it was. He is said to have murmured under his breath, as he put his name to the lie: *E pur si muove.* ("And yet it moves.") It was from the teaching of the Spanish Muslim Universities that Columbus got his notion that the world was round, though he too was forced by persecution to recant it afterwards. When we remember that the Spanish Muslim Universities in the time of the Khalifa Abdur Rahman III, and the Eastern Muslim Universities in the time of Al Ma'mun—I mention these two Monarchs because it is specially recorded of their times—welcomed Christian and Jewish students equally with Muslims—not only that, but entertained them at the Government expense; and that hundreds of Christian students from the South of Europe and the countries of the East took advantage of that chance to escape from ecclesiastical leading strings; we can easily perceive what a debt of gratitude modern European progress owes to Islam, while it owes nothing whatsoever to the Christian Church, which persecuted, tortured, even burnt the learned.

Let us now turn to Art.

Painting and sculpture were restricted by universal consent to conventional designs, because of the association of the forms of living creatures with idolatrous worship. There is no direct command that I can discover either in the Quran or in our Prophet's recorded sayings; only he refused the request of a Persian painter to be allowed to paint his portrait and take it back to show the Persian people, for fear lest it might be idolised. It is only in loose Persia and the countries under Persian influence, and after the decadence of Islamic civilisation had set in, that portrait and genre painting flourished among Muslims; and though the artistic results were in some cases remarkable, they cannot be classified as Islamic. For the same reason—their association with idolatrous worship—music and the drama came to be discouraged and despised arts. Though the delight of the common people kept music in existence it was regarded as an accessory of feasting, hardly as an art. The only singers in the Muslim world who were respectable were the Muezzins; these were honoured and were highly paid when they could be persuaded to sing at social gatherings, and sang a higher class of music than the common singers. There was music and song all through the Muslim world in the great days, but it was the music of men who strum the lute and sing for pleasure, not the ponderous art of music known to modern Europe.

As for the drama, it was also disregarded from the idea that it was beneath the dignity of a Muslim to dress up and pretend to be what he was not, and utterly beneath the honour of a Muslim woman. It was left at a low level, in the hands of strolling players, Greeks and Armenians.

5-A

The only thing approaching drama which was usual in the Muslim world was the shadow plays. These were given at all public and domestic festivals, covered a great variety of themes, and were brought to such perfection that the most intelligent could take delight in them. It is this sort of performance that is referred to in the famous Rubaîyah of Umar Khayyâm, which in Fitzgerald's translation runs :

"We are no other than a moving row of magic shadow-"shapes that come and go round with the sun-illumined "lantern held in midnight by the master of the show."

And the word Khayyâm, "tent-maker," reminds us of another art highly developed in the Muslim civilisation, the adornment of the inside of tents with many coloured arabesque designs and texts in intricate embroidery. The Khayyamîn, the tent-makers—St. Paul, a highly educated Jew, was one of them—you will remember were not mere tradesmen, they were artists of much skill and fancy.

I myself have witnessed many of the shadow plays— they were still going in Asia Minor, Syria and Egypt in the nineties of last century and though they were then quite relegated to the common herd, I can testify to the skill with which they were displayed and to the wit and wisdom of the showmen. They were indeed among the most amusing performances I have ever witnessed. It is only in the early nineteenth century that there was any sign of a real drama in the Muslim civilisation. Then in Persia and in Turkey some good plays were written, but not performed, by Muslims.—The performers were Armenians or Jews—and some really stirring plays which rank as literature were written by a learned Sheykh of Damascus upon subjects culled from Muslim life and history. I recall " Salâh-ud-din ul Ayyubi, " a historic drama on the grand scale, and a most touching and poetic little play verse called " Afifeh."

The position which the favourite actor fills in Modern Western Civilisation was filled in the Muslim Civilisation by the famous story-teller. A wonderland of stories, marvellous and quaint, exciting, interesting, always amusing, sometimes instructive, often true to life, was woven round the people's daily business by this class of artists. The product of their art, even since it has been gathered into books, has never in the East held rank of literature, though here and there a learned man, with conscious effort, has, *as a jeu d 'esprit*, stooped to raise it for a moment to that rank, as in the case of that peculiarly Arabian type of fiction known as Maqâmat. " Maqâmah " has nearly the same meaning as " Samar ", which is the name given to the stories which delight the common folk. Both words mean sitting up at night for entertainment. But "Maqâmah" applies to sittings up for entertainment in the mansions of the great, whereas " samar " refers to sitting-up for entertainment in the public coffee-houses or at corners of the street. Both " Maqamât" and " Samar " were still in vogue in Cairo and Damascus when I first knew them. Al-Harîrî took the idea of his great work, his Maqâmat, and even the name of his great rascal hero, Abu Zeyd, from the story-cycle of Abu Zeyd al Hajjâzi which was in the repertory of the strolling story-tellers. The cycle which is the best known is that of the Thousand

and one Nights, which people in the West regard as the great work of Arabic literature.

Wilfrid Blunt, in " The Stealing of the Mare," translated part of the story-cycle of the Abu Zeyd above mentioned. But there are many other story-cycles, as voluminous, and which have of recent years been published in Arabic—that of 'Antar, the pre-Islamic hero poet, for example, who has been called the Hercules of Arabia, and that of Seyf bin Zi Yazal, the patriarch who brought the Nile to Cairo, and no end of others.

The romance of 'Antar is a literary production if tradition tells the truth. It is said that there was once a shocking scandal in the palace of the ruler of Egypt, and all the people in the streets of Cairo kept clustering together to whisper about it. In order to give them something else to think of, the Ruler ordered a clever writer of the time to compose a story and distribute it to the public story-tellers. He chose the legend of 'Antar, the Arabian hero, the poet whose fine poem beginning

هل غادرالشعرآءً من متردم   أم هل عرفتالدا ربعد توهم

is among the seven Golden Odes of Arabia. He wrote the story in numbers, each number ending at a most exciting moment. These he gave out to the story-tellers, one by one ; and the story-tellers recited them at night to those who gathered round their flaming torches. Soon, we are told, the scandal in the ruler's palace was forgotten absolutely. The people took the keenest interest in these narrations. It is told of a man who had heard part of the story of 'Antar told in a street of Damascus centuries after its first publication in Cairo, that he could not sleep that night for thinking of poor 'Antar in the hands of his enemies, the Persians, and wondering how he could escape. The story-teller had left off at a most exciting point, just like a modern serial-story-writer. In the end he went and roused the story-teller and by promising him money, induced him to recite the next instalment of the story to him in the middle of the night. And so his mind had rest. These compositions on the borderland of folk-lore and literature were regarded in the Muslim world with amusement but some measure of contempt, as the pasture of comparatively ignorant and light-minded people. But we of the modern world cannot so despise them since to them can be clearly traced the origin of the most important form of literature in the West in modern times—the art of fiction.

In Architecture.... What is left for me to say about the achievements of the Muslim civilisation in the field of Architecture? From the Cathedral of Cordova to the square of Samarcand, from the Alhambra to the Taj Mahal, from the little Saint's tomb which crowns the high hill overlooking Pesth across the Danube to the cupolas of Kairouan and Cairo and the Dome of the Rock at Jerusalem—which a learned German has lately called the most glorious monument to be found on earth to-day—there are as many styles of architecture as there are countries in Islamic history, and all are Islamic, and all can show examples which all nations must admire. Mosques, palaces, castles, schools, hospitals, pleasure-houses, and above all gardens—there is no end to the variety of the paradise which Islamic architecture has created for the lover of beauty. The Muslims of the great days were lovers of beauty before everything—beauty of shape, beauty of intricate design, beauty of colour—and because the forms associated with idolatrous worship were denied to them, they consentrated all the more upon the beauties of nature. Their works are in subtle harmony with nature, they never clash with their natural surroundings. The beauty of their vaulted buildings. and their great covered bazaars is like that of mighty caverns of the hills or the sea shore, and objects in them have the shimmer of things seen in depths of water. Coolness in the shadow, colour in the sunshine, strength, majesty and power combined with grace and delicacy. These are the marks of Muslim architecture the world over. There were never such magnificent patrons of architecture, never such makers of gardens, or such beautifiers of landscape, as the Arab Caliphs or the Turkish Sultans or the Moghul Emperors. You all know the story of the Taj Mahal. But some of you may not know the story of Mo'tamid, King of Seville, and what he did to give his living wife a little pleasure. Because his lady 'Iamâd had once while travelling admired a snowstorm on the mountain-tops, Mu'tamid planted the whole hill above Cordova with almond trees that she might see it clothed in snow of blossom every spring. No-one who has ever seen them will forget the beauty of the Turkish and the Persian gardens, which I include under architecture because like the old Greek gardens, they are planned architecturally.

The art of caligraphy elaborated into intricate designs is peculiar to the Muslim world, as may be gathered from the name we give it—" Arabesque "—and very beautiful.

It is entirely due to the restriction on the art of painting. The same is true of the mosaics of beautifully coloured tiles, and exquisite flower and leaf designs in stone which distinguish Muslim architecture.

In Arabia, before the coming of Islam, there was only one form of literary composition—the poetic. The pagan Arabs excelled in poetry, and many Orientalists, on the strength of the Saba' Mudhahabât—the seven Golden Odes—incline to rank the few known poets of the Ignorance above all the hundreds and thousands of poets of the Muslim period. That is the view of men who prefer the music of the Shepherd's reed to that of a fine Orchestra. I think I am of those who do prefer it. There is a pathos in the few examples of the poetry of the Ignorance—the best—which very strongly appeals to me, but from the point of view of range and culture there is no possible comparison between the work of Imru'l—Qais or 'Antar or Ka'b ibn Zuhair, for example and that of Abu't—Tayyib Al Mutanabbi or of any other of the greater Muslim poets. In the Muslim civilisation poetry was not a gift of the Gods to a chosen few; it was the pastime and delight of all intelligent men. The mere names of the Arab poets and the Persian poets and the Turkish poets who have left behind them verses of high merit would fill several books.

I leave out from this survey the translated work of ancient Greek and Latin authors and the commentation on it, which filled multitudes of famous books, though these have been of signal service to humanity, carrying the torch of ancient learning for the West over a gulf of a thousand years; but they cannot be claimed as products of Islamic civilisation. Works on Ethics abound, and form a class of literature, largely conventional in form and contents, of which the Arabs were particularly fond, their fondness being largely for the stately cadence of the words. Rhetoric and logic of an academic kind filled many books, which, however, are generally unattractive to the modern reader. Works of Philosophy abound, all of them interesting, many of them—as, for instance, those of Al-Ghazzali—worthy of the closest study even now.

History was a science highly cultivated by the Muslims. It was ordinarily, as in Europe, an array of dates and wars and dynasties arranged for the convenience of the student's memory. But there are any number of historical works of a different character, giving intimate details, throwing light on human nature and contemporary manners, free of thought and wide of outlook. Among the Arabic writers of history who have charmed me, I must mention first " 'Umârah " the gossiping historian of the wars between Zabîd and Sana'a in the Yaman, next the Kitab-ul-Fakhri, then Ibn-ul-Athîr, and then Ibn Khaldûn whose view of history is so very modern that it is difficult to remember, when reading him, that he lived some centuries ago. Nor must I forget the voluminous but most interesting Ahmad-al-Jabarti, the historian of Egypt at the time of the French occupation and Arnaît Muhammad Ali's rise to power. These are what Europeans would call secular historians.

There is, besides, the great class of historians who treat exclusively of the history of Islâm. Among the more sober of these, I love Ismail Abu'l Fidâ, and among the more fantastic Majad-ud-dîn, the historian of the holy city of Jêrusalem.

Then there are the many books of travel, of which Ibn Batûtah's is the best known today, but by no means the most useful or interesting.

I now come to classes of literature which have no counterpart outside the countries of Islam. The vast number of collections of the Sayings of the Holy Prophet, with or without comments. The peculiarity of this class of literary work is its meticulous eagerness to check and verify, to admit nothing that is not authentic. The work of the early collectors was revised and sifted by collectors of another age, authorities in every case were given and if a tradition seemed imperfectly supported, it was labelled " Weak." There are six collections which Sunni Muslims accept as authentic, the best known being Sahîh-ul-Bukhâri and Sahîh Muslim.

Then there is that other great volume of literature—perhaps the greatest—which is included under the heading " Fiqh " or Muslim Jurisprudence, which includes the laws of statecraft, the political and social laws, and rules of daily conduct, with a wealth of illustration which enlightens it; as well as the rules of 'ibâdat (worship) down to the way to fold one's arms and place one's feet and bow one's head in prayer, and the exact degree of intimacy that a man should observe with his wife. This peculiar science is a product of the ecclesiasticism or scholasticism which I have shown to be the cause of the decay of Muslim Institutions. The object of its authors was to show the sufficiency of the Quran without the light of this world. It errs in exalting the letter and neglecting the spirit, and contains much that to a modern mind, seems very trifling. But it is not negligible, much less despicable.

It charts the detailed exploration of a field of knowledge which is absolutely necessary to the Muslims if they would succeed. Just as in the pursuit of Alchemy men lighted on the truth of chemistry; so in the pursuit of a false aim, the segregation of Islam, the restoration of the barrier between secular and religious which Islam abolished, the learned professors of *fiqh* throughout the centuries have garnered up and classified for us the whole treasure of Islamic teaching. Only one thing—the recognition that these laws were never static, but dynamic—is required to make of Fiqh the richest portion of our Muslim heritage.

Then there is another very large class of literature entirely concerned with Arabic Grammar, which for Muslims ranks as one of the exact sciences—by no means a dull science, as you might suppose, but a very fascinating pursuit to which many Westerners who have touched it have been tempted to devote their lives. No other language of the peoples who embraced Islam has such an ancient, deeply rooted and enduring structure, therefore no other language can stand the close analysis to which Arabic has been and is still being subjected—without exhausting the material, that is the wonder of it. There are always new problems to be solved, and new discoveries to be made. The Turks alone have been able to adopt the Arabic Grammar to a large extent, and that is chiefly owing to their amazing system of verbs, and particularly gerunds. This science being closely connected with the study of the Holy Quran, and bringing light to bear upon that study, has always held high rank among Islamic peoples. Browning's glorification of the Grammarian in his poem, " The Grammarian's Funeral ", would be natural in a Muslim poet treating of an Arabic Grammarian. As compared with the elaborate science of the Arabs, we Europeans, most of all we English have no Grammar at all.

I have merely touched on a few salient points in this immensely interesting and vast subject. In conclusion I will name another class of literature—again a huge one and with many sub-divisions—I mean that which deals with Tasawwuf, the means by which a man in this world can make personal approach to God. Most modern Western writers seem to think that the existence of God is debateable. The Muslim does not think so, for his belief in God is based not on faith alone but also on his personal experience. And the Sûfi writers have described that experience with a critical exactness which would satisfy the Physical Research Society. In days when the Western world is so much interested in attempts to demonstrate the existence of the spirit world and establish relations with it, this natural science—for it is a science, and, I think, as natural as any other which aims at the improvement of man's status and enlargement of his mental vision—is one that deserves more notice than is generally given to it. Some of the best philosophy, the deepest thought and the most splendid poetry which Islamic culture has produced is to be found in this class of literature. I speak only of that portion of it that I know, which is the Arabic and Turkish portion. The Persian is more widely known and advertised, but the Arabs would reject much of it as too imaginative, and not characterised by the sobriety of thought and scientific accuracy proper to the treatment of so high a subject. Certain it is that many Sûfis of the Persian tradition have become schismatics and led men astray which has never been the case with those of the Arabic tradition. Indeed, Persia, though a land of gorgeous poetry and varied culture, has always been a source of false Islamic inspiration. The Persian mind seeks ecstacy even at the cost of truth, whereas the Arab and the Turkish mind seeks truth even at the cost of disillusionment. True Sûfism is the spirit as against blind worship of the letter of Islam, and the true Sufis have kept the spirit alive and pure through days when the majority of Muslims saw the letter only.

I would recommend the study of this scientific Sûfism —the sober Arab sort—especially to the European spiritualists who, in their search to find the evidences of life after death, aim low at intercourse with departed spirits. Study of this science would tell them that the only spirits of the dead which are in a position to answer to their call are the less fortunate whose sins attach them to this world for some time after they are disembodied. Study of this science might inspire in them a higher aim, and spare them many disappointments.

Muslim art and literature, even in the darkest period, has never died; but natural science was quite dead among the Muslims for about two centuries. Muslim literature began to revive about the middle of the nineteenth century. In Turkey, Syria and Egypt there has been a great revival with the spread of printing. I have already spoken in a former lecture of the very interesting modern literature of Turkey. In Egypt and Syria there has been a reblossoming of almost the whole field which we have just surveyed, from *fiqh* and *tasawwuf* on the one hand to the marvels of the story-tellers on the other, with the addition of any number of translations of the modern literary works of Europe, good, bad and indifferent. But the books which have had the greatest influence are books expounding the great laws of fiqh in reasonable style, especially the little masterpiece of Prince Said Halim Pasha, called in Turkish *Islamlashmaq* (" Islamise "), and translated from the Turkish into Arabic which sets forth what the modern State should be according to the Shari'ah, and tells the Muslims that their only way of revival is return to true Islam, since falling-off from true Islam has been their ruin. Here in India, also, we see a revival of Muslim literature centering around disputed points of *fiqh*. In Hyderabad, the foundations of a new era of culture associated with a new literary language—Urdu—which may come to be the fourth great language of Islam—have been well and truly laid by the great Muslim ruler whom it is my privilege to serve. Everywhere there are signs of the beginning of a great revival which, please God, will place Islam once more in a position to fulfil its mission in the world.

FIFTH LECTURE.

TOLERANCE.

There is a quality which one associates with a high degree of human culture, and that is tolerance. One of the commonest charges brought against Islam historically, and as a religion, by Western writers is that it is intolerant. This is turning the tables with a vengeance when one remembers various facts—one remembers that not a Muslim is left alive in Spain or Sicily or Apulia. One remembers that not a Muslim was left alive and not a mosque left standing in Greece after the great rebellion in 1821. One remembers how the Muslims of the Balkan peninsula, once the majority, have been systematically reduced with the approval of the whole of Europe, how the Christians under Muslim rule have in recent times been urged on to rebel and masacre the Muslims, and how reprisals by the latter have been condemned as quite uncalled for. One remembers how the Jews were persecuted throughout Europe in the Middle Ages; what they suffered in Spain after the expulsion of the Moors; what they suffered in Czarist Russia and Poland even in our own day; while in the Muslim Empire Christians and Jews had liberty of conscience and full self-government in all internal affairs of their communities.

In Spain under the Ummayad and in Baghdad under the Abbasid Khalifas, Christians and Jews, equally with Muslims, were admitted to the schools and Universities—not only that, but were boarded and lodged in hostels at the cost of the State. When the Moors were driven out of Spain, the Christian conquerors held a terrific persecution of the Jews. Those who were fortunate enough to escape fled, some of them to Morocco and many hundreds to the Turkish Empire, where their descendants still live in separate communities, and still speak among themselves an antiquated form of Spanish. The Muslim Empire was a refuge for all those who fled from persecution by the Inquisition; and though the position which the Jews and Christians occupied there was inferior to that of Muslims it was infinitely to be preferred to the fate of any Muslims, Jews or heretics—nay even any really learned and enlightened man—in contemporary Europe.

The Western Christians, till the arrival of the Encyclopædiats in the eighteenth century, did not know, and did not care to know, what the Muslims believed, nor did the Western Christians seek to know the views of Eastern Christians with regard to them. The Christian Church was already split in two, and in the end, it came to such a pass that the Eastern Christians, as Gibbon shows, preferred Muslim rule, which allowed them to practise their own form of religion and adhere to their peculiar dogmas, to the rule of fellow-Christians who would have made them Roman Catholics or wiped them out. The Western Christians called the Muslims pagans, paynims, even idolators—there are plenty of books in which they are described as worshipping an idol called Mahomet or Mahound, and in the accounts of the conquest of Granada there are even descriptions of the monstrous idols which they were alleged to worship—whereas the Muslims knew what Christianity was, and in what respects it differed from Islam. If Europe had known as much of Islam, as Muslims knew of Christendom, in those days, those mad, adventurous, occasionally chivalrous and heroic, but utterly fanatical outbreaks known as the Crusades could not have taken place, for they were based on a complete misapprehension. To quote a learned French author :

"Every poet in Christendom considered a Mohammadan to be an infidel and an idolator, and his gods to be three ; mentioned in order, they were Mahomet or Mahound or Mohammad, Opolane and the third Termogond. It was said that when in Spain the Christians overpowered the Mohammadans and drove them as far as the gates of the city of Saragossa, the Mohammadans went back and broke their idols. A Christian poet of the period says that Opolane the " god " of the Mohammadans, which was kept there in a den was awfully belaboured and abused by the Mohammadans, who, binding it hand and foot, crucified it on a pillar, trampled it under their feet and broke it to pieces by beating it with sticks ; that their second god Mahound they threw in a pit and caused to be torn to pieces by pigs and dogs, and that never were gods so ignominiously treated ; but that afterwards the Mohammadans repented of their sins, and once more reinstated their gods for the accustomed worship, and that when the Emperor Charles entered the city of Saragossa he had every mosque in the city searched and had "Muhammad" and all their Gods broken with iron hammers."

That was the kind of " history " on which the populace in Western Europe used to be fed. Those were the ideas which inspired the rank and file of the crusaders in their attacks on the most civilised peoples of those days. Christendom regarded the outside world as damned eternally, and Islam did not. There were good and tender-hearted men in Christendom who thought it sad that any people should be damned eternally, and wished to save them by the only way they knew—conversion to the Christian faith. The mission of St. Francis of Assisi to the Muslims, and its reception, vividly illustrate the difference of the two points of view. So does the history of the Crusade of St. Louis against Egypt, which also had conversion as its object. A very interesting illustration of this point is to be found among the records of the Society of Friends, commonly called the Quakers. It was the subject of an article by Mabel Brailsford in the Manchester Guardian in November 1912.

In Charles II's reign a young English woman, who had been a servant-girl, became an active member of the Society of Friends and suffered persecution on that account. She was twice flogged in England for protesting against Church customs of the day. She, with two other Quakers, went to preach in New England, as the American colonies were then called. There they were thrown into prison on a charge of witchcraft and released only after many hardships. After her return to England she set out with five other Quakers to convert the Grand Signior, as the Sultan of Turkey was called. In the journey across Europe her companions fell into the hands of the

6—A

Inquisition, and only one of them was ever heard of afterwards. He returned to England after many years, a gibbering madman. She after much persecution and annoyance, pursued her journey quite alone, took ship at Venice and was put ashore on the coast of the Morea, far from the place she wished to go to, but in Muslim territory. From thence she walked all the way to Adrianople, but she need not have gone on foot; for from the moment she set foot in the Muslim Empire persecution was at an end. Everybody showed her kindness; the Government Officials helped her on her way; and when she reached Adrianople, where the Sultan Bayazid was then encamped and asked for audience of the Emperor, saying that she brought a message to him from Almighty God, the Sultan received her in State, according her all the honours of an ambassador. He and his courtiers listened with grave courtesy to all she had to say, and, when she finished speaking, said it was the truth, which they also believed. The Sultan asked her to remain in his country as an honoured guest or, at least, if she must depart, to accept an escort worthy of the dignity of one who carried a message of the Most High. But she refused, departing as she had come, on foot and alone, and so reached Constantinople, without the least hurt or hindrance, and there took passage on a vessel bound for England. It was not until the Western nations broke away from their religious law that they became more tolerant; and it was only when the Muslims fell away from their religious law that they declined in tolerance and other evidences of the highest culture. Therefore the difference evident in that anecdote is not of manners only but of religion. Of old, tolerance had existed here and there in the world, among enlightened individuals; but those individuals had always been against the prevelant religion. Tolerance was regarded as un-religious, if not irreligious. Before the coming of Islam it had never been preached as an essential part of religion.

For the Muslims, Judaism, Christianity and Islam are but three forms of one religion, which, in its original purity, was the religion of Abraham:—Al-Islam, that perfect SELF-SURRENDER to the will of God, which is the basis of Theocracy. The Jews, in their religion, after Moses, limited God's mercy to their chosen nation and thought of His Kingdom as the dominion of their race.

Even Christ himself, as several of his sayings show— for instance, when he asked if it were meet to take the children's bread and throw it to the dogs, and when he declared that he was sent only to the lost sheep of the House of Israel—seemed to regard his mission as to the Hebrews only; and it was only after a special vision vouchsafed to St. Peter that his followers in after days considered themselves authorised to preach the Gospel to the Gentiles.

The Christians limited God's mercy to those who believed certain dogmas, and thought of His Kingdom on earth as a group apart from the main stream of this world's life—the aggregate of devout Christians. Every one who failed to hold the dogmas was an outcast or a miscreant, to be persecuted for his or her soul's good. In Islam only is manifest the real nature of the kingdom of God.

اِنَّ الَّذِينَ آمَنُوا وَالَّذِينَ هَادُوا وَالنَّصَارَي وَالصَّابِئِينَ مَنْ آمَنَ بِاللهِ وَالْيَوْمِ الاخِرِ وَعَمِلَ صَالِحًا فَلَهُمْ اجْرَهُمْ عِنْدَ رَبِّهِمْ وَلَاخَوْفٌ عَلَيْهِمْ وَلَاهُمْ يَحْزَنُونَ ·

" Verily those who believe, and those who keep the Jew's religious rule, and Christians, and Sabaeans —whosoever believeth in Allah and the Last Day, and doeth right—their reward is with their Lord; and there shall no fear come upon them, neither shall they suffer grief."

وَقَالُوا لَنْ يَدْخُلَ الْجَنَّةَ الَّا مَنْ كَانَ هُودًا اوْ نَصَارَي تِلْكَ امَانِيهِمْ قُلْ هَاتُوا بُرْهَانَكُمْ انْ كُنْتُمْ صَادِقِينَ · بَلَى مَنْ اسْلَمَ وَجْهَهُ لِلهِ وَهُوَ مُحْسِنٌ فَلَهُ اجْرُهُ عِنْدَ رَبِّهِ وَلَا خَوْفٌ عَلَيْهِمْ وَلَاهُمْ يَحْزَنُونَ ·

" They say; none entereth Paradise unless he be a Jew or a Christian. Such are their own desires. Say: Bring your proof (of that which ye assert) if ye are truthful.

Nay, but whosoever surrendereth his purpose to Allah while doing good (to men), surely his reward is with his Lord; and there shall no fear come upon them, neither shall they suffer grief."

And again:

وَقَالُوا كُونُوا هُودًا اوْ نَصَارَي تَهْتَدُوا قُلْ بَلْ مِلَّةَ ابْرَاهِيمَ حَنِيفًا وَمَا كَانَ مِنَ الْمُشْرِكِينَ - قُولُوا آمَنَّا بِاللهِ

وما انزل الينا وما انزل الي ابراهيم واسماعيل واسحاق
ويعقـوب والاسبـاط وما اوتي موسـي وعيسـي وما اوتي
النبيـون من ربهم لا نفرق بين احـد منهـم ونحن لـه
مسلمون ـ فان آمنوا بمثل ما آمنتم بـه فقـد اهتـدوا
وان تولـوا فانمـاهـم في شقـاق فسيـكفيـكهم الله
وهـو السميـع العليـم .

"They say : Be Jews or Christians then will ye
be rightly guided. Say : Nay, but (ours is)
the religion of Abraham, the man by nature
upright, and he was not of those who ascribe
partners (to Allah).

"Say : We believe in Allah and in that which is
revealed unto us, and that which was revealed
to Abraham and Ishmael and Isaac and the
tribes, and that which was given to Moses and
Jesus and that which was given to the Prophets.
We make no difference between any of them,
for we are those who have surrendered (unto
Him).

"And if they believe in the like of that which ye
believe, then are they already rightly guided ;
and if they are averse, then are they in opposition.
Allah will suffice thee (for defence) against
them. He is All-Hearing, All-Knowing."

And yet again :

الله لا الـه الا هو الحي القيـوم لا تاخذه سنـة ولا
نوم لـه مافي السموات ومافي الارض من ذا الذي يشفـع

عنـده الا باذنـه يعلم مابين ايـديهم وماخـلفهـم ولا
يـحـيـطـون بشيـي مـن علمـه الا بمـا شـاء وسـع
كرسيـه السـمـوات والارض ولايؤده حـفـظهـمـا
وهوالعلي العظيم ـ لا اكراه في الدين قـد تبين الرشـد
مـن الغـي فـمـن يـكفـر بالطـاغـوت ويومـن باللـه
فقـد استمسـك بالعروة الوثـقي لاانـفصام لهـا واللـه
سميـع عـليـم ·

" Allah ! There is none to be worshipped save
Him, the Alive, the Enduring. Age and slum-
ber come not nigh Him. His is all that is in
the heavens and that all that is in the earth.
Who is he that intercedeth with Him save by
His leave ? He knoweth all that is in front of
them and all that is behind them, while they
encompass nothing of His knowledge save what
He will. His throne extendeth beyond the
Heavens and the Earth, and He is never weary
of preserving them. He is the Sublime, the
Tremendous.

" There is no compulsion in religion. The right
direction is henceforth distinct from error. And
who so rejecteth vain superstitions and believeth
in Allah hath grasped a firm handle which will
not give way. Allah is all-Hearing, All-Knowing.'

The two verses are supplementary. Where there is
that realisation of the majesty and dominion of Allah,
there is no compulsion in religion. Men choose their

path—allegiance or opposition—and it is sufficient punishment for those who oppose that they draw further and further away from the light of truth.

What Muslims do not generally consider is that this law applies to our own community just as much as to the folk outside, the laws of Allah being universal; and that intolerance of Muslims for other men's opinions and beliefs is evidence that they themselves have, at the moment, forgotten the vision of the Majesty and mercy of Allah which the Qurân presents to them.

But people will object that Muslims to-day are very intolerant people, who call everybody who does not agree with them a Kâfir, an infidel. And many Muslims even will, alas! seek to justify such abuse by saying that in the Qurân itself there are many references to the Kâfirîn as people with whom the Muslims ought to have no dealings, people upon whom they should wage war. At the risk of wearying my audience I shall pause to explain who and what the Kâfir really is.

In the Qurân I find two meanings, which become one the moment that we try to realise the divine standpoint. The Kâfir, in the first place, is not the follower of any religion. He is the opponent of Allah's benevolent will and purpose for mankind—therefore the disbeliever in the truth of all religions, the disbeliever in all Scriptures as of divine revelation, the disbeliever to the point of active opposition in all the Prophets whom the Muslims are bidden to regard, without distinction, as messengers of Allah. The first of the Kâfirîn was Iblis (Satan)—

the angel who through pride refused to pay reverence
to Man when he was ordered to do so.

واذ قلنا للملائكة اسجدوا لآدم فسجدوا الا
ابليس ابي واستكبر وكان من الكافرين .

"And when We said unto the angels:
Prostrate yourselves before Adam,
they fell prostrate all except Iblis.
He refused through pride, and so
became of the disbelievers." (Kâfirîn).

The Quran repeatedly claims to be the confirmation
of the truth of all religions. The former Scriptures had
become obscure, corrupted; the former Prophets appeared
mythical, so extravagant were the legends which were
told concerning them, so that people doubted whether
there was any truth in the old Scriptures, whether such
people as the Prophets had ever really existed. Here—
says the Qurân—is a Scripture whereof there is no doubt;
here is a Prophet actually living among you and preaching
to you. If it were not for this Book and this Prophet,
men might be excused for saying that Allah's guidance
to mankind was all a fable. This Book and this Prophet,
therefore, confirm the truth of all that was revealed before
them, and those who disbelieve in them to the point of
opposing the existence of a Prophet and a revelation are
really opposed to the idea of Allah's guidance—which
is the truth of all revealed religion.

قل من كان عدوا لجبريل فانه نزله علي قلبک
باذن الله مصدقاً لما بين يديه وهدي وبشري

للمومنـين - من كان عـدوا للـه وملائـكتـه ورسـله
وجبـريـل وميكال فان اللـه عـدو للـكافـرين .

" Say : Who is an enemy to (the angel) Gabriel ?
For he it is who hath revealed (this Scripture)
to thy heart, confirming all that was revealed
before it, and for a guidance and glad tidings
to believers.

" Who is an enemy to Allah and to His angels
and His messengers and Gabriel and Michael ?
Verily Allah is an enemy to disbelievers (in
His guidance)."

In those passages of the Holy Qurân which refer to
warfare, the term Kâfir is applied to the actual fighting
enemies of Islam. It is not applicable to the non-Muslim
as such, nor even to the idolator as such, as is proved by a
reference to the famous Proclamation of Immunity from
obligations towards those faithless tribes of the idolators
who, after having made treaties with the Muslims, nad
repeatedly broken treaty and attacked them :

بـراءة مـن اللـه ورسولـه الي الـذين عـاهدتم
مـن المشركيـن فسيـحـوا في الارض اربعـة اشهر واعـامـوا
انـكم اغير معـجـزي اللـه وان اللـه مـخـزي الـكافـرين -
واذن مـن اللـه ورسولـه الي الناس يوم الحج الاكبـر
ان اللـه بـرىء مـن المشركيـن ورسولـه فان تبتـم فهـو خير
لـكم وان تـوليتـم فاعـامـوا انـكم غيـر مـعـجـزي اللـه
وبشـر الذين كفروا بعـذاب اليم - الا الذيـن عـاهدتم

7

من المشركين ثم لم ينقصو كم شيئاً ولم يظاهروا
عليكم أحدا فاتموا اليهم عهدهم الى مدتهم
ان الله يحب المتقين .

"(A statement of) immunity from Allah and
His messenger towards those of the idolators
(Mushrikin, not Kâfirn) with whom ye made
a treaty (but they broke it).

"So travel freely in the land four months and
know that ye cannot weaken Allah, and that
Allah will abase the opponents (Kâfirîn).

"And a proclamation to the people on the day of
the greater pilgrimage that Allah and his messenger are free from obligations towards the
idolators (Mushrikîn). So if ye repent it will
be best for you, but if ye turn away, then know
that ye cannot weaken Allah. Warn those
who oppose hereafter (O Muhammad) of a painful punishment.

"Except those of the idolators (Mushrikîn) with
whom you have a treaty, and who have not
injured you in aught, ror aided anyone against
you. (As for them), fulfil their treaty perfectly
until the term thereof. Lo! Allah loveth those
who keep their duty (unto Him)."

Here it is evident that a distinction is drawn between
mushrikin (idolators—literally, those who attribute partners to Allah) in general, and the Kâfirîn. The idolators
who kept faith with the Muslims were not Kâfirîn. Our
Holy Prophet himself said that the term Kâfir was not

to be applied to anyone who said " Salâm " (peace) to the Muslims. The Kâfirs, in the terms of the Qurân, are the conscious evil-doers of any race or creed or community.

I have made a long digression but it seemed to me necessary, for I find much confusion of ideas even among Muslims on this subject, owing to defective study of the Quran and the Prophet's life. Many Muslims seem to forget that our Prophet had allies among the idolators even after Islam had triumphed in Arabia, and that he " fulfilled his treaty with them perfectly until the term thereof." The righteous conduct of the Muslims, not the sword, must be held responsible for the conversion of those idolators, since they embraced Islâm before the expiration of their treaty.

So much for the idolators of Arabia, who had no real beliefs to oppose to the teaching of Islâm, but only superstition. They invoked their local deities for help in war, and put their faith only in brute force. In this they were, to begin with, enormously superior to the Muslims. When the Muslims nevertheless won, they were dismayed; and all their arguments based on the superior power of their deities were for ever silenced. Their conversion followed naturally. It was only a question of time with the most obstinate of them.

It was otherwise with the people who had a respectable religion of their own—the People of the Scripture ‫أهل الكتاب‬ . as the Quran calls them—*i.e.*, the people who had received the revelation of some former Prophet: the Jews, the Christians and the

Zoroastrians were those with whom the Muslims came at once in contact. To these our Prophet's attitude was all of kindness. The Charter which he granted to the Christian monks of Sinai is extant. If you read it you will see that it breathes not only goodwill but actual love. He gave to the Jews of Medina, so long as they were faithful to him, precisely the same treatment as to the Muslims. He never was aggressive against any man or class of men; he never penalised any man, or made war on any people, on the ground of belief, but only on the ground of conduct. The story of his reception of Christian and Zoroastrian visitors is on record. There is not a trace of religious intolerance in all this. And it should be remembered—Muslims are rather apt to forget it, and it is of great importance to our outlook—that our Prophet did not ask the people of the Scripture to become his followers. He asked them only to accept the Kingdom of Allah, to abolish priesthood and restore their own religions to their original purity. The question which, in effect, he put to everyone was this : ' Are you for the Kingdom of God which includes all of us, or are you for your own community against the rest of mankind?' The one is obviously the way of peace and human progress, the other the way of strife, oppression and calamity. But the rulers of the world, to whom he sent his message, most of them treated it as the message of either an insolent upstart or a mad fanatic. His envoys were insulted cruelly, and even slain. One cannot help wondering what reception that same embassy would meet with from the rulers of mankind to-day, when all the thinking portion of mankind accept the Prophet's premisses, have thrown off the trammels of priestcraft, and harbour some idea of human brotherhood.

قل يا اهل الكتاب تعالوا الي كلمته سوآء بيننا وبينكم الا نعبد الا الله ولا نشرك به شيئاً ولا يتخذ بعضنا بعضاً ارباباً من دون الله فان تولوا فقولوا اشهدوا بانا مسلمون .

"Say: O people of the Scripture come to a proposal of arrangement between us and you : that we shall worship none but Allah, and that we shall ascribe no partner unto Him, and that no one of us shall take another for Lord besides Allah. And if they turn away, then say: Bear witness that we are they who have surrendered (unto Him)."

If the people of the Scripture, thus appealed to, had agreed to this proposal they also would have been of those who have surrendered unto Allah (Muslimûn). The Messenger of Allah was not to seek his own aggrandisement; his sole concern was to deliver his message to the nations. A Unitarian Christian community would have been, for him, a Muslim community; and a Jewish community which rejected the priestcraft and superstition of the rabbis would have been the same.

But though the Christians and Jews and Zoroastrians refused his message, and their rulers heaped most cruel insults on his envoys, our Prophet never lost his benevolent attitude towards them as religious communities; as witness the charter to the monks of Sinai already mentioned. And though the Muslims of later days have fallen far short of the Holy Prophet's tolerance, and have sometimes shown arrogance towards men of other faith, they have always given special treatment to the Jews and Christians. Indeed the Laws for their special treatment form part of the Shari'ah.

In Egypt the Copts were on terms of closest friendship with the Muslims in the first centuries of the Muslim conquest, and they are on terms of closest friendship with the Muslims at the present day. In Syria the various Christian communities lived on terms of closest friendship with the Muslims in the first centuries of the Muslim conquest, and they are on terms of closest friendship with the Muslims at the present day, openly preferring Muslim domination to a foreign yoke.

There were always flourishing Jewish communities in the Muslim realm, notably in Spain, North Africa, Syria, Iraq, and later on in Turkey. Jews fled from Christian persecution to Muslim countries for refuge. Whole communities of them voluntarily embraced Islam following a revered rabbi whom they regarded as the promised Messiah, but many more remained as Jews, and they were never persecuted as in Christendom. The Turkish Jews are one with the Turkish Muslims to-day. And it is noteworthy that the Arabic-speaking Jews of Palestine—the old immigrants from Spain and Poland— are one with the Muslims and Christians in opposition to the transformation of Palestine into a national home for the Jews.

To return to the Christians, the story of the triumphal entry of the Khalifah Umaribn-ul-Khattab · رضي الله عنه into Jerusalem has been often told, but I shall tell it once again, for it illustrates the proper Muslim attitude towards the People of the Scripture. The general who had taken Jerusalem asked the Khal'fah to come in person to receive the keys of the Holy City. The Khal'fah travelled from Medina very simply, with only a single camel and a single slave. Master and man used the camel alternately, ride and tie. The astonishment of the gorgeous slave-officials of the Roman Empire when they saw the ruler of so great an empire coming in such humble guise may be imagined. None the less they paid him reverence and led him to the church of the Holy Sepulchre as the glory of their city. While 'Umar was in the Church the hour of Asr prayer arrived. The Christian officials urged him to spread his carpet in the Church itself, but he refused, saying that some of the ignorant Muslims after him might claim the Church and convert it into a mosque because he had once prayed there. He had his carpet carried to the top of the steps outside the church, to the spot where the Mosque of 'Umar now stands—the real Mosque of 'Umar, for the splendid Qubbat us—Sakhrah, which tourists call the Mosque of Umar, is not a mosque at all, but the temple of Jerusalem, a shrine within the precincts of the Masjid al Aksa, which is the second of the Holy Places of Islâm.

From that day to this, the Church of the Holy Sepulchre has always been a Christian place of worship, the only things the Muslims did in the way of interference with the Christian's liberty of conscience in respect of it was to see that every sect of Christians had access to it, and that it was not monopolised by one sect to the exclusion of others. The same is true of the Church of the Nativity at Bethlehem, and of other buildings of special sanctity. Under the Khulafa-ur-Râshidin and the Ummayads, the true Islamic attitude was maintained, and it continued to a much later period under the Ummayad rule in Spain. In those days it was no uncommon thing for Muslims and Christians to use the same place of worship. I could point to a dozen buildings in Syria which tradition says were thus conjointly used; and I have seen at Lud (Lydda), in the plain of Sharon, a Church of St. George and a mosque under the same roof with only a partition wall between. The partition wall did not exist in early days. The words of the Khalifah Umar proved true in other cases; not only half the Church at Lydda, but the whole church in other places was claimed by ignorant Muslims of a later day on the mere ground that the early Muslims had prayed there. But there was absolute liberty of conscience for the Christians; they kept their most important churches and built new ones; though by a later edict their church bells were taken from them because their din annoyed the Muslims, it was said; only the big bell of the Holy Sepulchre remaining. They used to call to prayer by beating a nâqûs, a wooden gong, the same instrument which the Prophet Noah is said to have used to summon the chosen few into his ark. The equality of early days was later marred by social arrogance on the part of the Muslims, but that came only after the Crusades. The Christians were never persecuted, save for a short period when Southern Syria was conquered by the Fatemites of Egypt for a time. Then, under the mad ascetic Khalîfah, Al-Hâkim bi amr Illah (whom the Durûz to this day worship as God incarnate) they suffered very cruel persecution. Hundreds of Christian hermits living in caves among the rocks of the Judaean wilderness were ordered to be abominably mutilated, and though they escaped through the intervention of the local Muslims, cruel persecution of the Christians did take place; their pilgrims were interfered with, and the services of the Church of the Holy Sepulchre were interrupted for a time. It was the news of that persecution, carried to Europe by returning pilgrims which was the cause of the first Crusade. But by the time the Crusading army reached Syria, the Fatemites had been driven out and the condition of the Christians was again normal.

It was not the Christians of Syria who desired the Crusades, nor did the Crusaders care a jot for them, or their sentiments, regarding them as heretics and interlopers. The latter word sounds strange in this connection, but there is a reason for its use. The great Abbâsid Khalîfah Hârûn-ar-Rashîd had, God knows why, once sent the keys of the Church of the Holy Sepulchre among other presents to the Frankish Emperor, Charlemagne. Historically, it was a wrong to the Christians of Syria, who did not belong to the Western Church, and asked for no protection other than the Muslim Government. Politically, it was a mistake and proved the

7-A

source of endless after trouble to the Muslim Empire. The keys sent, it is true, were only duplicate keys. The Church was in daily use. It was not locked up until such time as Charlemagne, Emperor of the West, chose to unlock it. The present of the keys was intended only as a compliment, as who would say: " You and your people can have free access to the Church which is the centre of your faith, your goal of pilgrimage, whenever you may come to visit it." But the Frankish Christians took the present seriously in after times, regarding it as the title to a freehold, and looking on the Christians of the country as mere interlopers, as I said before, as well as heretics.

That compliment from King to King was the foundation of all the extravagant claims of France in later centuries. Indirectly it was the foundation of Russia's even more extortionate claims, for Russia claimed to protect the Eastern Church against the encroachments of the Roman Catholics; and it was the cause of nearly all the ill-feeling which ever existed between the Muslims and their Christian Zimmis. When the Crusaders took Jerusalem they massacred the Eastern Christians with the Muslims indiscriminately, and while they ruled in Palestine the Eastern Christians, such of them as did not accompany the retreating Muslim army, were deprived of all the privileges which Islam secured to them and were treated as a sort of outcastes. Many of them became Roman Catholics in order to secure a higher status; but after the re-conquest, when the emigrants returned, the followers of the Eastern church were found again to be

in large majority over those who owned obedience to the
Pope of Rome. The old order was re-established, and all
the Zimmis once again enjoyed their privileges in accordance with the Sacred Law. But the effect of those
fanatical inroads had been somewhat to embitter Muslim
sentiments, and to tinge them with an intellectual contempt, for Christians generally; which was bad for
Muslims and for Christians both ; since it made the former
arrogant and oppressive to the latter socially, and the
intellectual contempt, surviving the intellectual superiority,
blinded the Muslims to the scientific advance of the West
till too late. The arrogance hardened into custom, and
when Ibrâhïm Pasha of Egypt occupied Syria in the third
decade of the nineteenth century, a deputation of the
Muslims of Damascus waited on him with a complaint
that under his rule the Christians were beginning to ride
on horseback. Ibrâhïm Pasha pretended to be greatly
shocked at the news, and asked leave to think for a whole
night on so disturbing an announcement. Next morning,
he informed the deputation that since it was, of course, a
shame for Christians to ride as high as Muslims, he gave
permission to all Muslims thenceforth to ride on camels.
That was probably the first time that the Muslims of
Damascus had ever been brought face to face with the
absurdity of their pretentions.

By the beginning of the eighteenth century A.D., the
Christians had, by custom been made subject to certain
social disabilities, but these were never, at the worst, so
cruel or so galling as those to which, the Roman Catholic
nobility of France at the same period subjected their own
Roman Catholic peasantry, or as those which Protestants

imposed on Roman Catholics in Ireland; and they weighed only on the wealthy portion of the community. The poor Muslims and poor Christians were on an equality, and were still good friends and neighbours. The Muslims never interfered with the religion of the subject Christians. There was never anything like the inquisition or the fires of Smithfield. Nor did they interfere in the internal affairs of their communities. Thus a number of small Christian sects, called by the larger sects heretical, which would inevitably have been exterminated if left to the tender mercies of the larger sects whose power prevailed in Christendom, were protected and preserved until to-day by the power of Islam.

Innumerable monasteries, with a wealth of treasure of which the worth has been calculated at not less than a hundred millions sterling, enjoyed the benefit of the Holy Prophet's charter to the monks of Sinai and were religiously respected by the Muslims. The various sects of Christians were represented in the Council of the Empire by their patriarchs, on the provincial and district councils by their bishops, in the village councils by their priests; whose word was always taken without question on things which were the sole concern of their community. With regard to the respect for monasteries, I have a curious instance of my own remembrance. In the year 1908 the Arabic congregation of the Greek Orthodox Church in the Church of the Holy Sepulchre, or Church of the Resurrection as it is locally called, rebelled against the tyranny of the Monks of the adjoining convent of St. George. The convent was extremely rich, and a large part of its revenues

were derived from lands which had been made over to it
by the ancestors of the Arab congregation for security
at a time when property was insecure; relying on the
well-known Muslim reverence for religious foundations.
The income was to be paid to the depositors and their
descendants, after deducting something for the convent.
No income had been paid to anybody by the Monks for
more than a century, and the congregation now demanded
that at least a part of that ill-gotten wealth should be
spent on education of the community. The Patriarch
sided with the congregation, but was captured by the
Monks, who kept him prisoner. The congregation tried
to storm the convent, and the amiable monks poured
vitriol down upon the faces of the congregation. The
congregation appealed to the Turkish Government, which
secured the release of the Patriarch and some concessions
for the congregation, but could not make the monks
disgorge any part of their wealth because of the immuni-
ties secured to Monasteries by the Sacred Law. What
made the congregation the more bitter was the fact that
certain Christians who, in old days, had made their property over to the Masjid—Ul-Aksa—the great mosque
of Jerusalem—for security, were receiving income yearly
from it even then.

Here is another incident from my own memory.
A sub-prior of the Monastery of St. George purloined a
handful from the enormous treasure of the Holy Sepulchre
—a handful worth some forty thousand pounds—and
tried to get away with it to Europe. He was caught at
Jaffa by the Turkish customs officers and brought back

to Jerusalem. The poor man fell on his face before the Mutasarrif imploring him with tears to have him tried by Turkish Law. The answer was: "We have no jurisdiction over monasteries," and the poor grovelling wretch was handed over to the tender mercies of his fellow-monks.

But the very evidences of their toleration, the concessions given to the subject people of another faith, were used against them in the end by their political opponents just as the concessions granted in their day of strength to foreigners came to be used against them in their day of weakness, as Capitulations.

I can give you one curious instance of a "capitulation," typical of several others. Three hundred years ago, the Franciscan friars were the only Western European missionaries to be found in the Muslim Empire. There was a terrible epidemic of plague, and those Franciscans worked devotedly, tending the sick and helping to bury the dead of all communities. In gratitude for this great service, the Turkish Government decreed that all property of the Franciscans should be free of customs duty for ever. In the Firmân the actual words used were "Frankish (i.e., Western European) missionaries " and at a later time, when there were hundreds of missionaries from the West, most of them of other sects than the Roman Catholics, they all claimed that privilege and were allowed it by the Turkish Government because the terms of the original Firmân included them. Not only that, but they claimed that concession as a right, as if it had been won for them by force of arms or international treaty instead of being, as it was, a free gift of the Sultan; and called upon their consuls and ambassadors to support them strongly if it was at all infringed.

The Christians were allowed to keep their own languages and customs, to start their own schools and to be visited by missionaries of their own faith from Christendom. Thus they formed patches of nationalism in a great mass of internationalism or universal brotherhood; for as I have already said the tolerance within the body of Islam was, and is, something without parallel in history, class and race and colour ceasing altogether to be barriers.

In countries where nationality and language were the same as in Syria, Egypt and Mesopotamia there was no clash of ideals, but in Turkey, where the Christians spoke quite different languages from the Muslims, the ideals were also different. So long as the rationalism was unaggressive, all went well; and it remained unaggressive—that is to say, the subject Christians were content with their position—so long as the Muslim Empire remained better governed, more enlightened and more prosperous than Christian countries. And that may be said to have been the case, in all human essentials, up to the beginning of the seventeenth century. Then for a period of about eighty years the Turkish Empire was badly governed; and the Christians suffered not from Islamic Institutions but from the decay or neglect of Islamic Institutions. Still it took Russia more than a century of ceaseless secret propaganda work to stir up a spirit of aggressive nationalism in the subject Christians, and then only by appealing to their religious fanaticism.

After the eighty years of bad Government came the era of conscious reform, when the Muslim Government turned its attention to the improvement of the status of all the peoples under it. But then it was too late to win back the Serbs, the Greeks, the Bulgars and the Rumans. The poison of the Russian religious-political propaganda had done its work, and the prestige of Russian victories over the Turks had excited in the worst elements among the Christians of the Greek Church, the hope of an early opportunity to slaughter and despoil the Muslims, strengthening the desire to do so which had been instilled in them by Russian secret envoys, priests and monks.

I do not wish to dwell upon this period of history, though it is to me the best known of all, for it is too recent and might rouse too strong a feeling in my audience. I will only remind you that in the Greek War of Independence in 1821, three hundred thousand Muslims—men and women and children—the whole Muslim population of the Morea without exception, as well as many thousand in the northern parts of Greece—were wiped out in circumstances of the most atrocious cruelty; that in European histories we seldom find the slightest mention of that massacre, though we hear much of the reprisals which the Turks took afterwards; that before every massacre of Christians by Muslims of which you read, there was a more wholesale massacre or attempted massacre of Muslims by Christians; that those Christians were old friends and neighbours of the Muslims—the Armenians were the favourites of the Turks till fifty years ago—and that most of them were really happy under

Turkish rule, as has been shown again and again by their tendency to return to it after so-called liberation.

It was the Christians outside the Muslim Empire who systematically and continually roused their religious fanaticism : it was their priests who told them that to slaughter Muslims was a meritorious act. I doubt if anything so wicked can be found in history as that plot for the destruction of Turkey. When I say " wicked," I mean inimical to human progress and therefore against Allah's guidance and His purpose for mankind. For it has made religious tolerance appear a weakness in the eyes of all the worldlings, because the multitudes of Christians who lived peacefully in Turkey are made to seem the cause of Turkey's martyrdom and downfall ; while on the other hand the method of persecution and extermination which has always prevailed in Christendom is made to seem comparatively strong and wise. Thus religious tolerance is made to seem a fault, politically. But it is not really so. The victims of injustice are always less to be pitied in reality than the perpetrators of injustice. From the expulsion of the Moriscoes dates the degradation and decline of Spain. San Fernando was really wiser and more patriotic in his tolerance to conquered Seville, Murcia and Toledo than was the later king who, under the guise of Holy warfare, captured Granada and let the Inquisition work its will upon the Muslims and the Jews. And the modern Balkan States and Greece are born under a curse. It may even prove that the degradation and decline of European civilisation will be dated from the day when so-called civilised statesmen agreed to

8

the inhuman policy of Czarist Russia and gave their
sanction to the crude fanaticism of the Russian Church.
There is no doubt but that, in the eyes of history, religious
toleration is the highest evidence of culture in a people.
Let no Muslim, when looking on the ruin of the Muslim
realm which was compassed through the agency of those
very peoples whom the Muslims had tolerated and protected through the centuries when Western Europe thought
it a religious duty to exterminate or forcibly convert
all peoples of another faith than theirs—let no Muslim,
seeing this, imagine that toleration is a weakness in Islam.
It is the greatest strength of Islâm because it is the attitude
of truth. Allah is not the God of the Jews or the Christians or the Muslims only, any more than the sun shines
or the rain falls for Jews or Christians or Muslims only.
Still, as of old, some people say :

لن يدخل الجـنفـة الا من كان هودا او نصاري.

"None enters Paradise except he be a Jew or a
Christian."

Answer them in the words of the Holy Quran :

بلي من اسلم وجهه لله وهو محسن فله اجره
عند ربه ولا خوف عليهم ولا هم يحزنون.

"Nay but whosoever surrendereth his purpose
towards God, while doing good to men, surely
his reward is with his Lord, and there shall
no fear come upon them, neither shall they suffer
grief."

SIXTH LECTURE.

THE CHARGE OF FATALISM.

I have shown you something of Islamic culture in
s splendour and decline. It is the fashion to ascribe
s decline to a certain defect said to be inherent in Islam :
s fatalism. To what then one must ascribe the rise of
slamic culture, the leading position which the Muslims
ttained and long maintained in the world ? Logically,
his too must be ascribed to fatalism if fatalism is inherent
Islam. Which is impossible! And how are we to
ccount for the indubitable fact that Muslims showed
ost energy, and so won most success, while they obeyed
he precepts of their religion strictly and with full intelli-
ence, and became languid and declined in proportion
s they disobeyed its precepts and obscured their mean-
g if fatalism is indeed a defect and inherent in Islam ?
t all hinges on the old question of predestination and
ee will which has agitated the Christian world, as it has
gitated the Muslim world, at certain periods of history.
n the Qurân, the province of freewill is clearly indicated.
t is but a province in the midst of Allah's Sovereignty
nd even in that province man cannot escape from Allah's
w of consequences.

اين ما تكونوا يدرككم الموت ولوكنتم في بروج
مشيدة وان تصبهم حسنة يقولوا هذه من عندالله
وان تصبهم سيئة يقولوا هذه من عندك قل كل من
عندالله فمال هؤلاء القوم لا يكادون يفقهون حديثا

ما اصابك من حسنة فمن اللـه وما اصابك من
سيئة فمن نفسك وارسلناك للناس رسولا وكفي بالله
شهــيــدا .

> "Wheresoever ye may be death will overtake you,
> even though ye be in lofty towers. And if
> good befalleth them they say: This is from
> Allah, and if ill befalleth them they say: This is
> from thee (O Muhammad). Say: All is from
> Allah. What aileth these people that they can-
> not come near to understand a plain fact.

> "Whatever of good befalleth thee (O man) it is
> from Allah, and whatever of ill befalleth thee it
> is from thyself. We have sent thee (O Muham-
> mad) as a messenger to men. And Allah is
> sufficient witness."

Those are the two verses of the Qurân round which
this controversy of predestination and freewill has chiefly
raged, and at a glance they seem to contradict each other
But they refer to a particular reverse which befell the
Muslim arms, in which some men were killed; and when
that is known, and the nature of the murmuring among
the Muslims, most of the difficulty disappears. Death
is a matter over which no man has control, and which
is certain sooner or later to overtake all of us. And man
is subject to vicissitudes of fortune which also are upon
him from Allah. The Prophet was only a man, therefore
it was folly for the people to blame him for such
vicissitudes. "What aileth these people that they canno
even come near to understand a plain fact?" The plain

fact, often reiterated in the Quran, is that Muhammad (صلعم) was a man, and not a supernatural being. The present misfortune was due to secret disaffection or dissension in the Muslim ranks, a thing forbidden by Allah. Victory had been theirs when they were obedient to Allah. Therefore it is said: Whatever of good befalleth thee (O man) it is from Allah, and whatever of ill befalleth thee it is from thyself (through disobedience). The Prophet cannot change God's Law of consequences.

That there is much fatalism in the teaching of Islam and in the example of the early Muslims is a fact. But it is not of the kind which the Western world ascribes to Muslims and is the reverse of laziness. The misapprehension comes largely from observation, and imperfect observation, of the Turks, a race of soldiers, who regarded war as a Muslim's business, and peace-time as furlough. It is strange that controversy should have singled out this passage which does not seem to me to touch the larger question of predestination and freewill so much as do a hundred other passages. It is a question, like the definition of eternity, which is quite beyond our understanding —one of those matters which we are warned in the Qurân itself to let alone, not seeking to expound them.

The position of mankind in the world is that of Allah's viceroy.

واذ قال ربك للملائكة اني جاعل في الارض خليفة قالوا اتجعل فيها من يفسد فيها ويسفك الدماء

ونحن نسبح بحمـدك ونقدس لك قال اني اعلم
مـالا تعلمـون .

> "When thy Lord said unto the angels : I am about
> to place a viceroy in the earth, they said : Wilt
> thou place therein one who will do evil therein
> and shed blood, while we, we hymn thy praise
> and sanctify thee. He said : I know that which
> ye know not."

While man recognises his dependence and regards
the powers that have been confided to him as a sacred
trust, of which he will some day have to render an account,
it is well with him. When he forgets or denies his dependence, he is in error and will come to grief. In the Sûrah
which is reported to have been the first revealed, we read :

كلا ان الانسان ليطغي ـ ان رأءه استغني ـ ان الي
ربك الرجعي .

> "Nay. but verily man is rebellious
> "That he deemeth himself independent
> "Verily unto thy Lord is the return."

Man is given charge of this world, with all its animals
and trees and plants; and his duty is to cultivate and
improve it for the good of all mankind, not to devastate
and despoil it for his own pleasure. He has been given
charge, within plain limits, of his fellow-man, and his
duty is to cultivate and improve himself and others and
pave the way for the advance of future generations. His
absolute dependence on the natural laws which govern
all existence : his inability to breathe or raise an arm
without obeying laws he never made; the spectacle

of day and night; the laws of growth and decay and new growth, of birth and death; the law of consequences which attends on all his acts—all these should be a perpetual reminder to man that his sovereignty or province of freewill is strictly bounded, and always at the mercy of an infinitely greater power. But they often fail to remind him of this plain fact, and then " man is rebellious and deemeth himself independent " and evil and corruption grow apace.

The position of the Muslims in the world is that of men and women pledged to make known this truth, and strive unceasingly for the establishment of Allah's Kingdom, which means universal brotherhood. The Qurân does not limit Allah's Kingdom to a race or sect. The test of loyalty is not the recitation of a certain creed, or the performance of a certain set of ceremonies. The test is one for all mankind, and it is *Conduct*. The Muslim has to strive for good, wherever found, against evil, wherever found. His surrender to the purpose of Allah, in realisation of His Kingship, does not lead to a state of motionless contemplation or of lethargy. It is the beginning of a life of conscious effort, which, however, brings no pain to him, but rather great relief and gladness; just as the swimmer who has struggled long against the tide feels when the tide has turned and now supports him. This strife for good against evil of the Muslim, beginning in himself, extending to his fellow-men and ending, it may be in death upon the battlefield, is called *Jihâd*.

In Jihâd, the Muslim leaves all things to God's mercy and cares not for death, nor when and where it may

befall him. This is the real fatalism of the **Muslims**; but it is not a fatalism which could ever cause stagnation and decay. It was when the Muslims lost the spirit of Jihâd in works of peace, and lost sight of the larger meaning of the term in the restricted meaning which the scholiasts attached to it, that Muslim civilisation began to stagnate.

Never was the narrowing of the meaning of a word down from the world-wide to the technical, which has been the process of scholasticism in Islam, more evident, or more disastrous in its consequences, than in this case of Jihâd. Among non-Muslims it was commonly supposed to mean war for the conquest of anybody and everybody who profess any religion other than Islam—a fanatical outbreak analogous to that denoted by the word Crusade. Even among Muslims it has come to be accepted as meaning war for the defence of Islam; so much so that the War Department of the Sultân-Khalîfa and his Viceroy, the Khedive of Egypt, was called not النظارة الحربية the Ministry of War, but النظارة الجهادية, the Ministry of Jihâd, it being a pious fiction that wars waged by the authority of the supreme head of the Islamic brotherhood must always be in the nature of Jihâd.

This pious fiction was necessary for the army authorties, because, according to the Sacred Law, the Muslims can be called upon to fight only in a war which has the nature of Jihâd. Thus a standing order for conscription could only be justified by the fiction that all the wars in which the army would take part would have that nature—*must* have that nature since they were waged with the authority of the Khalîfah of the Muslims which pre-supposed the fatwah of the Sheykh-ul-Islâm who represented all the learned in religious law. In old days, when the Muslim Universities were at the height of their power and influence, the learned in the Sacred Law judged independently, distinguished clearly between Jihâd warfare and wars of mere ambition or self-interest, and unanimously and invariably condemned the latter as totally unsanctioned by the Sharî'ah. They could not altogether stop the warfare of ambitious rulers, but they imposed restrictions which made it harmless to the peoples as a whole. Thus no ruler might force any free Muslim to assist him in such warfare, or levy any public tax for such a purpose. A ruler wishing to make war upon another ruler must do so at his personal expense, with the help of slaves bought with his own money and such others as might join him of their own free will. He and his army must not touch the life or occupation of the peaceful Muslims. Any wrong done to the peaceful Muslims —' the quiet people,' as they called them, was punished by the 'Ulama, who could rouse the whole Muslim world against the delinquent. So such wars did practically no injury whatever to the civilisation or solidarity of the Muslims. The quiet people saw the fighting slaves go by to battle and went on with their daily work. It mattered not to them who won, for change of rulers meant no revolution. The Sacred Law was one for all the Muslims, and whoever ruled was bound to obey it; since the 'Ulama were there to shame him in the eyes of the whole world if he did not. In the same way the 'Ulama of old condemned warfare against non-Muslims

8-A

in which the ground of action for the Muslims was not that of manifest right against manifest wrong. If all the wars waged by all Muslims throughout history had been on the plane of Jihâd, as were the wars waged by the early Muslims, Islâm would have been the religion of the world today, and the world would have been in a healthier condition spiritually and morally than it now is.

Wars which fall under the heading of Jihâd can be fought only in self-defence, for the protection of the weak who are oppressed, and the redress of wrongs. Non-combatants must not be harmed, priests and religious institutions have to be respected, crops must not be laid waste, fruit-bearing trees must not be cut down.

" Destroy not their means of subsistence."

That was the Prophet's Law against his enemies. Compare it with the law of modern Europe as exhibited in the late War, when it was considered quite legitimate to seek by every means to starve the enemy, and choose which you prefer. The Prophet's aim was to reduce the horrors of war, to render it comparatively mild, and its results so beneficial to the conquered that the hearts of men should be drawn towards Islâm, and so peace should dawn for the world. There was, in his time, not a trace of that idea, which did prevail at times among the Muslims afterwards, that it was a sacred duty to wage war on unbelievers.

Everyone who sought peace with the early Muslims could obtain it and, so long as he kept faith with them,

had equal rights. Their respect for treaties was proverbial. The Qurân makes every contract sacred; and the
Muslims have preserved their fair renown in this respect.
Jihâd warfare was a part of Islamic culture which modern
nations would do well to study and to imitate. The
Prophet, in his warfare, several times forgave his enemies,
with wonderful results.

There is, of course, one thing which the out-and-out
pacifist will always object to in Islamic teaching, and that
is the command to fight in self-defence, for the protection
of the weak and helpless, and for the redress of wrong—
the plain command to kill, in certain circumstances. This
command has been made the subject of atrocious calumnies
against Islam. Mr. Lloyd George at the Genoa Peace
Conference, and a learned judge in India about the same
time, quoted these words from the Quran:

" Kill them wherever you find them"
apart from their context, as if they were an order to the
Muslims to murder and to massacre non-Muslims. In
their context no one could ascribe that meaning to them.
I quote the whole passage of the Holy Quran:

وقاتلوا في سبيل الله الذين يقاتلونكم ولا تعتدوا
ان الله لا يحب المعتدين - واقتلوهم حيث ثقفتموهم
واخرجوهم من حيث اخرجوكم والفتنة اشد
من القتل ولا تقاتلوهم عند المسجد الحرام حتي يقاتلوكم
فيه فان قاتلوكم فاقتلوهم كذلك جزاء الكافرين -
فان انتهوا فان الله غفور رحيم - وقاتلوهم حتي لا تكون

فتنة ويكون الدين كله لله فان انتهوا فلا عدوان الا
على الظالمين .

"Fight in the way of Allah against those who
fight against you, but begin not hostilities.
Lo! Allah loveth not aggressors.

"And kill them wherever you find them and drive
them from the places whence they drove you
out; for persecution is worse than killing. And
fight not with them at the sanctuary (of Mecca)
till they attack you there, and if they attack
you kill them. That is the reward of graceless
people.

"But if they desist, then verily Allah is Forgiving,
Merciful.

"Fight against them till there is no more persecution and religion is all for Allah; but if they
desist, then let there be no hostility except
against wrongdoers."

This is no command to murder and massacre. It
is simply the ordinary rule of War put in plain terms
to men who until then had thought it wrong to take life
under any circumstances. For the Muslims until then
had been strict pacifists. And they were to fight against
others, not to enforce on others their belief, but for freedom
of belief against men who wished to uproot Islam, and
were persecuting Muslims with that object. They were
to fight until there should be no more persecution, till the
Quranic principle of لا اكراه في الدين "No compulsion
in religion" should be established, and religion should be

all for Allah (that is, should be free for all alike, since Allah is one for all, and has no favourites; till the only test should be the natural and fair test of conduct). I ought not to have to say it to any audience in the world—but the ignorance which prevails is so abysmal that I must proclaim it: There is, not one word in the Holy Qurân to justify murder or massacre under any circumstances whatsoever. All there is is a command for open, honourable warfare, under certain plain conditions, and with limitations which made Islamic warfare, by its mercy as compared with other warfare, a great factor in the success of Islam as a religion: for it surprised the peoples used to utter ruthlessness in war.

Warfare is only one, and that the extremest, form of Jihâd. Jihâd means effort or endeavour. In the religious sense, it properly applies to the whole effort of the Muslim to assert and establish the sovereignty of God in men's minds, by performing his religious duty as laid down in the Qurân—an effort which should last through all his life, should govern every action of his life, or he is no true Muslim. This duty may be summarised as the fight for good against evil in every connection and in every field, beginning with a man's own heart and mind.

Our Holy Prophet said :—

الجـهـاد الاكبر جهاد الهوى .

"The greatest Jihâd is that against a man's own lust;"

which means that the best way of recommending the belief in Allah's universal sovereignty and extending the new realm of peace and brotherhood was by the example of their righteous conduct. The term *Al-Jihâd ul-Akbar*, "The greatest Jihâd," is also applied by the Holy Prophet to the effort of the student to become learned and the effort of the learned to spread knowledge.

> "The ink of the scholar is more holy than the blood of the martyr."

The term Jihâd is also applicable to the effort of the faulty towards perfection, to the effort of those who do not fly from pestilence but stay to tend the sick and bury the dead, to active charity, to patience under persecution—indeed, to every form of human effort which aims at improvement, the defence of right and the redress of wrong. Trade was Jihâd, for the merchants went forth in the spirit of Jihâd as missionaries proud of their honourable dealing, their fidelity to contracts, carrying the truths of the Qurân to every place they visited even as the Arab merchants do today. It is therefore incorrect to limit the meaning of the term to warfare, much more to warfare of the fanatical religious kind; though every Muslim—indeed every man—worthy of the name, must be prepared to die, if need be, for the cause which he considers right. So little has Jihâd in common with the war-aims of that school of patriotism which holds that a man should be prepared to fight and die, if need be, for his country, **right** *or wrong* that our Prophet plainly said:

> "He is not of us who sides with his tribe in injustice, and he is not of us who summons others to aid him in aggression, and he is not of us who dies while assisting his tribe in tyranny."

He once astonished his companions by saying: "Help your Muslim brother when he is doing right and when he is doing wrong." They said: "What! Must we help him when he is doing wrong?" The Holy Prophet answered: "Yes, especially when he is doing wrong. Drag back his hand!"

The Muslims are those who only fight " in the way of Allah " (as it is called in the Quran), that is, in self-defence or for the protection of the weak oppressed, or for the redress of wrongs. To wage aggressive war on people, simply on account of their religious opinions, is not allowed, nor can the term Jihâd by any means be stretched to cloak such warfare. Jihâd is "striving in the way of Allah," and the way of Allah, if we must seek a modern phrase to express it, is devotion to the cause of human progress. It is only when a nation or community does grievous wrong to Muslims, attempting to exterminate or enslave them, and extinguish truth by force of arms, that war against them is a duty for all Muslims. Though Jihâd, this general effort after good, is charged on Muslims as a sacred duty, they have not to think of their effort as in any way needed by Allah, or as a help to Him.

ومن جاهد فانما يجاهد لنفسه ان الله لغني عن العالمين .

" Whosoever striveth, striveth for his own good, for Allah hath no need of His creatures."

There are English proverbs pointing to the same truth: " Virtue is its own reward." " God helps those who help themselves, and so on"; but the higher spiritual meaning of such pellets of old wisdom for collective humanity has never been so brightly illustrated as in the history of the early Muslims. For the result of this unselfish effort after goodness of a host of men, led and inspired by the example of a man, was the happiest civilisation that the world has known, and it remained the happiest until the effort was relaxed.

فان مع العسـر يسـرا ان مع العسـر يسـرا فاذا
فـرغت فانصب ـ والي ربـك فارغب ٠

" For verily with hardship cometh ease.
Verily with hardship cometh ease.
So when thou art relieved, still strive.
And seek to please thy Lord."

The Muslims of a later day forgot this truth, and when they were relieved from warfare and the evident need for effort relaxed their effort and so lost their ease. And so the Muslim civilisation lost its vigour and gradually sank into its long decline.

The vigorous but simple discipline of Islâm, always self-discipline—so unintelligible to outsiders who cannot conceive why any man or woman should do anything. not pleasure-giving and not profitable in a worldly sense, which he is not obliged to do—becomes intelligible when considered in connection with Jihâd. this unselfish effort for which men and women require training. The daily prayers, the yearly fast, the pilgrimage become but empty forms without the spirit of Jihâd. The Muslim cannot hope to be justified by faith alone nor by observance of the Sacred Law alone. The followers of other religions have been told: Believe only. The Muslims are commanded to Believe and Do—belief in God without right conduct being a fault and not a virtue, like a duty unperformed. The test is conduct.

It has been said by divines of a sister religion that a man has no duty towards himself. He has a duty towards God and a duty towards his neighbour. His duty towards himself is lost in those two duties. Islam has put it to us in another way. It does recognise a man's duty towards himself, and that duty is Jihâd, this striving for good against evil, beginning with the conquest of a man's own lusts. This duty of a man towards himself includes the duty to make war in certain circumstances, but it is none the less Jihâd though he be never called on to make war in all his life. His training for Jihâd is not only military training, it is the whole structure of Islamic discipline. Upon the other hand, universal military training is the natural corollary of the command to fight, and it must always be the law in an Islamic State. Every Muslim ought to be a trained Mujâhid, qualified to bear his part in the Jihâd which is for ever going on against the powers of evil, whether in his own conscience, or in the work-shop, or in the market-place, or in the council-chamber, or upon the battle-field. He ought never to become so absorbed in his temporal possessions or occupations that it would break his heart to be deprived of them or torn from them suddenly. He should be prepared, the moment that his possessions or his settled, peaceful life bring him into disobedience to the divine commands,

9

to resign them, or to change their nature or to emigrate, without reluctance, much less the despair which among the wordly would accompany such resignation.

انا لله وانا اليه راجعون ٠

"For we are Allah's, and unto Him we are returning."

It is but a little while, in any case, before we shall be obliged to leave behind us all that we have loved and valued in this world. What do we take with us ? Nothing. But we shall find something waiting for us, and by that we shall be judged for good or ill. It is

ما قدمت ايدينا ٠

"That which our own hands have sent before us," in the words of the Qurân—the record of the efforts we have made in the cause of righteousness, for the defence of Allah's Kingdom upon earth, on behalf of the weak, the ignorant, the poor, the suffering and the oppressed, and for the redress of wrongs. It is the account of our Jihâd. The wealth of this world is the gift of Allah. He bestows it upon whom He will and he removes it from whom He will. It is given always as a trust, often as a test of principle, sometimes as a trial, sometimes even as a punishment. It is a dangerous and troublesome possession, spiritually speaking, and it is insecure. What can we count on as secure ? Only the promise of Allah, that those who believe and those who strive for righteousness and those who leave their homes and their most loved possessions for the sake of Allah,

فلهم اجرهم عنـد ربهم ولا خـوف عـليهـم ولاهم
يـعـزنون .

" Their reward is with their Lord, and there shall
no fear come upon them, neither shall they suffer
grief."

This is the fatalism of Islam. But it is not the sort
of fatalism of which it is generally accused. It is a condition of vigorous, unceasing effort, and intense vitality.
Indeed the condition of Jihâd is glorious, ennobled life,
and it is easily within the reach of every one.

Now the impact of a different civilisation has con-
founded the ideas of the majority of Muslims, many of
whom are inclined to withdraw from it, as being based
on greed and usury instead of sacrifice, and seek their
own salvation as a folk apart. They perceive no religious
sanction for most of the pursuits of men today. Commerce has become a cut-throat, lying business, law mere
chicanery and science is being used for selfish and destructive purposes. In short, in the words of the Qurân

ان الانسان ليطغي - ان راء ها استغني .

" Man is rebellious
" That he thinketh himself independent."

But that is not a reason for the Muslims to withdraw from life, but the reverse, since to bring men back
to knowledge of the sovereignty of Allah is the very reason
why Islam was brought into existence. It is a simple
question of adjusting the idea and practice of Jihâd to
modern conditions, and that can be done only by the
revival of Islamic institutions in a modern guise. If

the existing modern society is based on usury, let Muslims
show an example of a modern society which is not based
on usury. If law is mere chicanery, let Muslims re-establish and obey the Sacred Law in all things which concern
their own community. If the present banking system
seems usurious to them, let them start a Muslim banking
system founded upon brotherhood, let them re-establish
Zakâh and Beyt-ul-Mâl. If existing commercial methods
strike them as villanous, let them set up their own commerce on co-operative lines. If the industrial system
seems to them a selfish tyranny, let them start their
own industrial system in accordance with the Sharî'ah.
It would be suicidal for the Muslims to become merged
in the new civilisation, for that would mean that they
accepted what they consider to be evil in it, and so could
never in this world again become a power for good. But
it would be equally suicidal for them to hold aloof from
it, when it contains the knowledge and efficient standard
of the present day. Muslims cannot go on living in the
past or they will lose Islam as surely as they would if
they accepted a non-Muslim civilisation unreservedly.
The Jihâd-ul-Akbar for the earnest Muslims today is
to obtain modern education so that they can discriminate
between what is good and what is noxious in the new era.
They must accept and assimilate what is good; and as
for what is evil, they must oppose to it some better thing
which may replace it in the course of time. If the world
is going to the devil, they alone can save it, for they alone
possess the standard by which civilisation should be judged,
and they alone are able to produce a complete alternative
system of civilisation, claiming the divine sanction—

a system which has worked with wonderful success in time past and, being adaptable to the needs of any age, may reasonably be expected to work with wonderful success in time to come; which cannot be said of all the schemes of Western revolutionaries which, so far, have, when put in practice, always failed to add a tittle to the sum of human happiness. And we must remember always that to strive for the success and triumph of our own community, right or wrong, against other communities, is not Jihâd. Jihâd is the strife for right against wrong, good against evil, wherever found. If you think that the ideal of such Jihâd has ever been absent from the Muslim world then you are wrong. Read of the dealings of the Ummayad and 'Abbâsid Khalîfas with the Roman Empire of the East, of the Spanish Ummayad Khalîfas with the Christian Kingdoms of the West: and you will see that their ideal was precisely this fight for right against wrong wherever found. Read the letter of Sultan Suleymân, the magnificent, to King Fiancis of France, when he was a prisoner and wrongfully despoiled of all his wealth, and you will see this principle set forth and strongly vindicated. Our aim is not to establish the empire of our own community, it is to establish the kingdom of God on earth; and the Sacred Law of Islam—containing natural laws which are for everybody—has the same wide human aim. To use it for a lower aim is to misinterpret it, and so court failure. Without the wider human aim there can be no Jihâd.

The 'Fatalism,' so much talked of, of the Muslims, is but recognition of the unavoidable. At the present day, it must be shown in cheerful acceptance of the existing conditions as the will of God; while their Jihâd, their religious effort, must be, as before, to strive for good against evil first in purifying and re-building the Islamic brotherhood on modern lines and then in seeking by their conduct and example to recall the world to conscience of God's universal sovereignty.

SEVENTH LECTURE.

THE RELATION OF THE SEXES.

Today I have to speak to you upon a delicate subject —the Islamic position of woman—a subject which is delicate, and to me painful, only because, at every turn when treating of it, I am reminded that I am in a country where, among the Muslims, woman is emphatically *not* in her Islamic position, and where men are generally indifferent to the wrongs done to her. The status to which the great majority of Muslim women in India are reduced today is a libel on Islam, a crime for which the Muslim community as a whole will have to suffer in increasing social degradation, in weak and sickly offspring, in increasing child mortality, so long as that crime is perpetuated. An unconscious crime on the part of the majority, I know, begun in ignorance, through pursuit of an un-Islamic tradition of false pride. But ignorance of the law is no excuse for anybody to escape its penalties—least of all, in the case of the operation of natural laws can the mere plea of ignorance exempt a man from undergoing the natural consequences of transgression. The laws of the Sharî'ah are natural laws, and the consequences of transgressing them are unavoidable, not for Muslims only, but for everyone. The fool who does not know that fire will burn him is burnt by fire, like anybody else. And the excuse of ignorance, in the case of Muslims and the Sharî'ah, is worse than the offence; since, they of all mankind, should have that special knowledge which it is their mission to convey to all mankind.

Please do not, hearing me thus inveigh against th
present pitiful condition of Muslim womanhood in India
think that I am judging it by any foreign standard o
wishing to recommend foreign ways. I am judging i
only by the Sharî'ah, and I wish to recommend only th
way of the Sharî'ah ; and I judge the Western status o
woman, as I judge her Eastern status, solely by th
Sharî'ah, as I, following the most learned and enlightene
Muslims of all ages, understand it.

وكذا لك جعلناكم امة و سطا لتكونـوا شهـداء
لي الناس ويكون الـرسول عليكم شهـيـدا .

> " Thus have we set you as a middle nation tha
> ye may bear witness against mankind and tha
> the Messenger may bear witness against you."

Surely the Messenger of Allah (may God bless an
keep him !) bears witness against you today in this matte
of the status and the rights of woman. Only recall hi
words !

طلب العلم فريضة علي كل مسلم ومسلمـة .

> " Education is a sacred duty for every Muslim an
> every Muslimah."

I know that an influential group of men among yo
have decided in their minds that عـلم (knowledge) must b
here taken in a restricted " theological " sense as meanin
only knowledge of a " religious " nature. The Hol
Prophet and the Holy Qurân never made distinction be
tween religious and secular. For the true Muslim the whol
of life is religious and the whole of knowledge is religious

And according to the proper teaching of Islam the man of widest knowledge and experience of life is the man best qualified to expound religious truth and solve the problems which arise among the Muslims in connection with the practice of religion. I deny the right of man of limited knowledge and outlook to exclusive interpretation. I deny their conclusions as I deny their premises. I say that their claim to exclusive interpretation amounts to priestly intervention between the Muslims and the Messenger whom Allah sent to them—a thing denounced in the Qurân repeatedly as against religion, and destructive of all true religion in the past. But I am willing to accept their restriction for the present. Let us agree for the sake of argument that علم means only what such people think it means, means only the knowledge which such men possess. Is every Muslimah in India encouraged or even allowed to seek such knowledge ? Does every Muslim woman in India receive that sort of education ? Does every Muslimah in India know even the Fâtihah, even the Kalimah ? Can every Muslimah in India say her prayers ? How many Muslimahs in India know the passages of the Qurân and the sayings of the Prophet which ought to govern the progressive evolution of woman's true position in the Muslim brotherhood ? Let them all be given that education, in God's name ! I ask no more as a beginning. All the rest will follow naturally.

Our Prophet (may God bless and keep him !) said : " Women are the twin halves of men." " The rights of women are sacred. See that women are maintained in the rights granted to them." Do Muslim women in India

9·A

know even what their rights are ? Equality with men
before the law is theirs according to the Sharî'ah. Women
have the right to their own property, have the right to
claim a divorce from their husbands under certain circumstances. How many Muslim women in India know that ?
And who is seeing that they are maintained in the rights
granted to them by the Sacred Law ? In India today,
women have no legal protector or defender. Where is
that woman Judge who, according to our great Imam Abu
Hanîfa ought to be in every city to deal particularly with
cases touching women's rights ? Where is the man Judge
to whom they have free right, and access to appeal ? The
Qadi used to be the guardian and defender of their rights.
His position in India today is almost as pitifully below his
true Islamic position as that of woman herself ; and one
sees as little reason why it should be.

Women have equal rights with men before the
Sharî'ah, and the Qurân proclaims that they are equal
with men in the sight of God. In the Holy Qurân God
says : " I suffer not the work of any worker among you,
whether male or female, to be lost. One is from the other."

The heathen Arabs thought of women as a separate
and inferior race. The Qurân reminds them they are all
one race, one proceeding from the other, the man from the
woman and the woman from the man.

There is no text in the Qurân, no saying of our Prophet,
which can possibly be held to justify the practice of de-
priving women of the natural benefits which Allah has
decreed for all mankind—sunshine and fresh air and healthy movement—or her life-long imprisonment causing the

death by consumption or anæmia of thousands of women every year ; and God knows how many babies ! Decency is enjoined by the Qurân, modesty is enjoined by the Qurân, the circle of a woman's intimate relations is prescribed by the Qurân, but nowhere in the Qurân or in our Prophet's teachings can you find authority for this. The true Islamic tradition, the pure Arabian tradition, enjoins the veiling of the hair and neck, and modest conduct— that is all. The veiling of the face by women is not, originally, an Islamic custom. It was prevalent in many cities of the East before the coming of Islam, but not in the cities of Arabia. The purdah system, as it now exists in India, was quite undreamt of by the Muslims of the early centuries ; who had adopted the face-veil and some other fashions for their women when they came into the cities of Syria, Mesopotamia, Persia and Egypt, at once as a concession to prevailing custom and as a protection to their women from misunderstanding by peoples accustomed to associate unveiled faces with loose character. Later on it was adopted even in the cities of Arabia as a mark of تمدّن a word generally translated "civilisation", but which in Arabic still retains a stronger flavour of its root meaning " townsmanship " than is carried by the English word. It has never been a universal custom for Muslim women, the great majority of whom have never used it; for the majority of the Muslim women in the world are peasants who work with their husbands and brothers in the fields. For them the face-veil would be an absurd encumbrance. The headveil, on the other hand, is universal.

The Egyptian, Syrian, Turkish or Arabian peasant-woman veiled her face only when she had to go into the town, and then it was often only a half-veil that she wore. On the other hand, when the town ladies went to their country-houses they discarded the face-veil, and with it nearly all the ceremonies which hedged their life in town. In no other country that I know of besides India do the customs which were adopted by the wealthiest townspeople for the safety and distinction of their women at a certain period—were adopted by people having spacious palaces and private gardens—apply to poor people who have only narrow rooms in which confinement of the women is sheer cruelty. And not everywhere did the wealthiest adopt those customs. 'Umârah tells us that among the Arabs of Al-'Yaman in the fifth Islamic century, the great independent chiefs made it a point of pride and honour never to veil the faces of the ladies of their families, because they held themselves too high and powerful for common folk to dare to look upon their women with desiring eyes. It was only the dynasty which ruled in Zabîd, and represented the Khilâfat of Bani'l-'Abbâs in Yaman which observed the haram system with some strictness, no doubt in imitation of the Persianised court of Baghdad.

Thus the purdah system is neither of Islamic nor Arabian origin. It is of Zoroastrian Persian, and Christian Byzantine origin. It has nothing to do with the religion of Islam, and, for practical reasons, it has never been adopted by the great majority of Muslim women. So long as it was applied only to the women of great houses, who had plenty of space for exercise within their palaces and had varied interests in life ; so long as it involved no cruelty and did no harm to women, it may be regarded as unobjectionable from the Islamic standpoint, as a custom of a period. But the moment it involved cruelty to women and did harm to them it became manifestly objectionable, from the point of view of the Sharî'ah, which enjoins kindness and fair treatment towards women, and aims at the improvement of their status. It was never applicable to every class of society and when applied to every class, as now in India, it is a positive evil, which the Sacred Law can never sanction.

The general condition of Muslim women in Turkey, Syria, Egypt and Arabia has always been emancipated as compared with their condition now in India. For instance, the town ladies of the middle class, wearing their veils, were free to go about, do shopping, visit other ladies. Indeed the world of women behind the veil was as free and full of interest as that of men, only it was separate from that of men, and largely independent of that of men. Women, duly veiled, were quite safe in the streets. Any insult offered to one of them was sufficient to rouse the whole Muslim population to avenge it. The women of the moderately well-to-do could come and go as they pleased and had no lack of social intercourse. The degree of freedom they enjoyed in divers countries was regulated by racial temperament and local traditions rather than Islamic Law, which merely guarantees to women certain rights—and there is no law in the world so fair to women —and lays down the principle that they are always to be treated kindly and their rights held sacred. For instance, there was a difference between the Arabs and the Turks in this respect, the Turks having adopted more of the Byzantine customs. But all that I have said applies to both. In neither of those races would the women have put up with the conditions in which the majority of Indian Muslim women live today ; and in neither of those races would the men have tolerated that condition for their women.

But even the condition of the Turkish woman of old days was found to have become a cruelty in modern times. The reason is so curious that I must give it. When the Turks first came to Anatolia and Rumelia they were a sallow-complexioned race from Central Asia, with slanting eyes and thin black beards, as portraits of the early Sultans and their generals show. That type is found to-day among the peasantry in the vilâyet of Adana, but hardly anywhere else. By centuries of intermarriage with the fair Circassians, Georgians, Syrians, Bulgars, Serbs, Albanians and other blond races of Asia and Europe, the Turks have now become as fair as English people. The change was marked by a terrible increase in the mortality of Turkish women, particularly by an increase in the numbers of the yearly victims of consumption. So long as the Turkish woman was of dark complexion, the languid, easy going life of the traditional Khânum Efendi did not harm her. But after she became of fair complexion she suffered visibly from the confinement—much less than that imposed on Indian Muslim ladies, but still a measure of confinement—of that life. The Turkish Doctors then discovered that blondes are generally weaker constitutionally than brunettes, and require a great deal more fresh air and physical exercise. When once the full significance of that discovery dawned on the rulers of Turkey, they became advocates of feminine emancipation and, with the ruthless logic of their race, abolished the face-veil and other unhealthy restrictions, as soon as ever they could.

The Turkish woman in the town now dresses as she has always dressed in the country, wearing the close fitting *bash urtu* (headveil) with a longer looser headveil over it, and a long loose mantle covering her form from head to foot—a dress much less coquettish, though more healthy, than the former black charshaf and face veil. She is encouraged to take exercise and to play games in the open air, for which special women's clubs have been started. She is receiving education equally with men, though separately from men. She is allowed to do things which would have scandalised her great-grandmothers. Yet it is all within the Sharî'ah, since the changed conditions made this enlargement of her sphere of free activity absolutely necessary for woman's health and happiness in these days. The changes have not been revolutionary for the Turkish ladies since they had always the example of the Turkish country folk before them to prevent them from confusing the town dress and town restrictions with the Sacred Law of Islam. The Turkish peasantry are very good Muslims indeed. Nowhere does one see Islamic rules of decency more beautifully observed than in the Turkish villages of Anatolia. Yet women in those villages and in Egyptian villages, and in Syrian villages, and in Circassian villages and in Arabian villages and among the Bedawi and other wandering tribes enjoy a freedom which would stupefy an Indian Maulvi.

It is the great misfortune of the Indian Muslims that they have no peasantry ; that they came into this land as conquerors, with ambitions and ideas befitting noblemen and rulers in Afghanistan and Turkistan and Persia in those days, so that now every Indian Muslim thinks it necessary for his *Izzat* to treat his women in. perhaps, a wretched hut as the original Bêg or Khân Sahib treated the women of his household or as the Mughal Emperor treated the women of his palace in the vast Zenâna quàrters of the fort at Agra. It is the lack of a peasantry which had made them confuse the purdah system of the wealthy townsfolk in the past with the Sacred Law of Islam. If there had been a Muslim peasantry in India, like the Muslim peasantry of Arabia, Egypt, Syria or Anatolia as the basis of the nation, the Indian Muslims could never have fallen into the error of supposing that the purdah system should be practised by the poor who dwell in hovels; and the rich would never have applied it both to town and country life. A peasantry has always common sense ; it has no absurd pretensions, no false standards. The peasant judges woman, as he judges man, by skill in work and skill in management. I have seen a woman govern an Egyptian village by sheer weight of practical good sense and character. The men obeyed her orders and were proud of her. That is no isolated instance. Yet the Egyptian fellâhîn are ardent Muslims, and observe Islamic regulations pretty strictly.

The laws of Islam with regard to the position of woman
are intended for the benefit of woman, for her health and
happiness and the improvement of her material and social
position; and they are not static, they are DYNAMIC.
They contemplate reasonable change as circumstances and
conditions change. They can never sanction any custom
that does injury or wrong to woman. The purdah system
is no part of the Islamic law. It is a custom of the court
introduced after the Khilâfat had degenerated from the
true Islamic standard and, under Persian and Byzantine
influences, had become a mere Oriental despotism. It
comes from the source of weakness to Islam, not from the
source of strength. The source of strength and of revival
to Islam has always been the peasant's farm, the black-
smith's forge, the shepherd's hut, the nomad herdsman's
tent. It was thence that fresh brains came to the schools,
fresh blood to the throne, fresh vigour to the camp, not
from the sort of people who enjoyed the purdah system.
Far better let the traces of a worn-out grandeur go; and
if the Muslims in India happen to be poor and forced to
work for a living, let them no longer feel ashamed to earn
it in the way that Islam considers honourable—by cultivation of the land. No country can ever in truth be called
a Muslim country of which the peasantry is non-Muslim.
And Muslims settled anywhere without a peasantry are
like a flower without a root. They cannot draw fresh
vigour from the soil.

I do not ask for any violent or sudden change. Edu-
cate women in obedience to our Prophet's plain command;
and, in the conditions of the present day, you will see this

10

un-Islamic purdah system vanished naturally. It has nothing whatever to do with Islamic rules of modesty and decency for men and women. These will remain unshaken—nay, they will be greatly strengthened—if the education which you give to men and women be sound Muslim education.

The Sharî'ah has nothing but benevolence for women; it favours their instruction and development. But it does not wish or expect them to assimilate themselves to men. Dr. Harry Campbell, lecturing before the institute of Hygiene in London lately, said : " Women have smaller lungs and fewer blood cells than men. In women the vital fire does not burn so quickly. It is thus obvious that women are not adapted like men for a strenuous muscular life. Mentally men and women differ in the realm of feeling rather than of intellect. Intellectually men and women stand somewhat upon the same footing. While genius is more common in the male sex, so also is idiotcy." There is therefore spiritual and intellectual equality, and physical difference, precisely as the Islamic law recognises. There is nothing in the Sharî'ah to give ground for the false ideas concerning woman's position in Islam which long prevailed and still prevail in Christendom. It is the spectacle of such a falling off from true Islamic standards as this in India which has led non-Muslims to declare that Muslims treat their women-folk like cattle, that Muslims hold that women have no souls.

It is true that the Western view of woman and the problem of the sexes, differs radically from the Muslim view in some respects, but not in the ways that Europeans usually imagine it to differ, nor in the way in which the conduct of too many Muslims makes it seem to the superficial observer to differ. By acting against the teaching of the Sharî'ah through ignorance—no Muslim worthy of the name would knowingly transgress the Sacred Law—we misrepresent Islam before the world ; our witness against mankind becomes false witness ; and the damage to the faith is thus incalculable. Most Muslims in India seem to be utterly unaware that Islam has furnished them with high ideals and a system in this matter of the relations of the sexes—ideals and a system well able to hold their own in argument as against the ideals and system, or lack of system, of the most modern and advanced of Western peoples. They cling to wretched un-Islamic customs, which are both irrational and anti-human, as if Islam were left without an argument in face of the emancipation of the West. Islamic marriage is not a sacrament involving bondage of the woman to the man, but a civil contract between equals terminable at the will of either party, though more readily at the man's will for reasons which were very cogent at the time when it was instituted and still have weight today. In India many Muslims seem to have adopted Hindu ideas of the status of woman in marriage, of widow remarriage and of inheritance, if all I hear is true. Again I would impress on you the fact that the injunctions of the Sacred Law cannot be neglected with impunity by anyone ; and also that they are not static, but dynamic. They point the way and give the impulse in the right direction ; they impose the limits which must be observed ; they trace the path which must be followed ;

but the details at a given period must be evolved, upon those lines, to suit the needs and circumstances of that period. Islam, the religion of human progress, never aims at stagnation or retrogression, or oppression or enslavement of the mind or body, but always at advance, at even justice, at emancipation.

It has been said that the Islamic view of woman is a man's view, while the Christian view of woman is a woman's view. One might add that, seeing that Christendom was always ruled by men, the Christian view has never been translated into terms of fact, but has merely caused confusion of ideas in theory and many inconsistencies in practice. Devotees of a sentimental ideal of divine womanhood are apt to underestimate the human value of the Muslim standpoint, and to talk as if Islam had lowered the social and moral position of Eastern women, and caused their personal degradation ; omitting altogether to take into account the fact that a minority of the womanhood of Christendom is degraded to a depth which every good Muhammadan surveys with horror while a larger number are debarred from all fulfilment of their natural functions, which the Muslim regards as a great wrong.

The historical truth is this : that the Prophet of Islam is the greatest feminist the world has ever known. From the lowest degradation he uplifted woman to a position beyond which she can go only in theory. The Arabs of his day held women in supreme contempt, ill-treated and

defrauded them habitually, and even hated them; for we
read in the Holy Qurân:

يا ايها الذين آمنوا لا يحل لكم ان ترثوا النساء
كرها ولا تعضلوهن لتذهبوا ببعض ما آتيتموهن الا ان
يأتين بفاحشة مبينة وعاشروهن بالمعروف فان
كرهتموهن فعسى ان تكرهوا شيئاً ويجعل الله فيه
خيرا كثيرا .

"Ye who believe! It is not allowed you to be heirs
of women against their will, nor to hinder them
from marrying, that you may take from them a
part of that which you have given them, unless
they have been guilty of evident lewdness. But
deal kindly with them, for if ye hate them it may
happen that ye hate a thing wherein Allah hath
placed much good."

The pagan Arabs regarded the birth of girl-children
as the very opposite of a blessing, and had the custom to
burry alive such of them as they esteemed superfluous.
The Qurân peremptorily forbids that practice, along with
others hardly less unjust and cruel. It assigns to women
a defined and honoured status, and commands mankind
to treat them with respect and kindness.

The Prophet said: "Women are the twin halves of
men." "When a woman observes the five times of prayer,
and fasts the month of Ramadhân, and is chaste, and is
not disobedient to her husband, then tell her to enter Paradise by whichever gate she likes."

"Paradise lies at the feet of the mother."

"The rights of women are sacred. See that women are maintained in the rights granted to them."

"Whoever does good to girls (children) will be saved from hell."

"Whoever looks after two girls till they come of age will be in the next world along with me, like my two fingers close to each other."

"A thing which is lawful, but disliked by Allah, is divorce."

"Shall I not point out to you the best of virtues? It is to treat tenderly your daughter when she is returned to you, having been divorced by her husband."

"Whoever has a daughter and does not bury her alive, or scold her, or show partiality to his other children, Allah will bring him into Paradise."

The whole personal teaching of the Prophet is opposed to cruelty, especially towards women. He said: "The best of you is he who is best to his wife." Innumerable are the instances of clemency in his recorded life. He forgave the woman who prepared a poisoned meal for him, from which one of his companions died, and he himself derived the painful, oft-recurring illness which eventually caused his death. The Qurân also on a hundred pages declares forgiveness and mercy to be better than punishment, whenever practicable—that is to say, whenever such forgiveness would not constitute a crime against humanity in the political sphere, or whenever, in the case of private individuals, the man or woman is capable of

real forgiveness, banishing all malice; otherwise the evil
would recur in aggravated form.

The Muslim view of woman has been so misrepresented
in the West that it is still a prevalent idea in Europe and
America that Muslims think that women have no souls!
In the Holy Qurân no difference whatever is made between
the sexes in relation to Allah; both are promised the same
reward for good, the same punishment for evil conduct.

ان المسلمين والمسلمات والمومنين والمومنات
والقانتين والقانتات والصادقين والصادقات
والصابرين والصابرات والخاشعين والخاشعات
والمتصدقين والمتصدقات والصائمين والصائمات
والحافظين فروجهم والحافظات والذاكرين الله كثيرا
والذاكرات اعدالله لهم مغفرة واجرا عظيما .

" Verily the men who surrender (to Allah) and women
who surrender, and men who believe and women who
believe, and men who obey and women who obey, and men
who are sincere and women who are sincere, and men who
endure and women who endure, and men who are humble
and women who are humble, and men who give alms and
women who give alms, and men who fast and women who
fast, and men who are modest and women who are modest,
and men who remember Allah much and women who
remember (Him), Allah hath prepared for them pardon
and a great reward."

It is only in relation to each other that a difference
is made—the difference which actually exists—a difference

of function. In a verse which must have stupefied the pagan Arabs, who regarded women as devoid of human rights, it is stated :

ولهن مثل الذي عليهن بالمعروف وللرجال عليهن درجة والله عزيز حكيم ·

> " They (women) have rights like those (of men) against them; though men are a degree above them. Allah is Almighty, All-Knowing."

The lot of poor widows was particularly hopeless in Arabia previous to the coming of Islam. The Holy Qurân sanctions remarriage of widows ; it legalises divorce and marriage with another husband, thus transforming marriage from a state of bondage for the woman to a civil contract between equals, terminable by the will of either party (with certain restrictions, greater in the woman's case for natural reasons, intended to make people reflect seriously before deciding upon separation) and by death. The Holy Prophet, when he was the sovereign of Arabia, married several widows, to destroy the old contempt for them, and to provide for them, as ruler of the State.

And that brings me to the old vexed question of polygamy. All Arabia was polygamous or rather I should put it, all Arabia recognised no legal or religious limits or restrictions to the treatment of women by men—before the coming of Islam. Islam imposed such limits and restrictions as transformed society. Fault is found with our religion by most Western writers because it does not enjoin strict monogamy ; and the very mission of Muhammad (may God bless and keep Him) has been questioned merely because he had more wives than one. I would point out that there is no more bright example of monogamic marriage in all history than the twenty-six years' happy union of our Holy Prophet with the lady Khadîjah. But that happy union was exceptional; and one might claim that happy marriage is exceptional, and that if our Prophet had had only that experience his usefulness as an example to mankind would have been less. He furnished an example of perfect monogamic marriage, and he also furnished an example of perfect polygamic marriage. Surely that was well, since the vast majority of men in those days were polygamists, and I really do not know that they have ceased to be so.

People sometimes talk as if polygamy were an institution of Islam. It is no more an institution of Islam than it is of Christianity (it was the custom in Christendom for centuries after Christ) but it is an existing human weakness to be reckoned with and in the interests of men and women (women chiefly) to be regulated. Strict monogamy has never really been observed in Western lands; but, for the sake of the fetish of monogamy, a countless multitude of women and their children have been sacrificed and made to suffer cruelly. Islam destroys all fetishes, which always tend to outcaste numbers of God's creatures. In Europe, side by side with woman-worship, we see the degradation and despair of women.

The Islamic system, when completely practised, does away with the dangers of seduction, the horrors of prostitution and the hard fate which befalls countless women and children in the West, as the consequence of unavowed polygamy. Its basic principle is that a man is held fully responsible for his behaviour towards every woman, and for the consequences of his behaviour. If it does away likewise with much of the romance which has been woven round the facts of sexual intercourse by Western writers, the romance is an illusion, and we need never mourn the loss of an illusion.

Take modern European literature—the most widely read—and you will find the object of man's life on earth depicted as the love of woman—in the ideal form as the love of one woman, the elect, whom he discovers after trying more than one. When that one woman is discovered the reader is led to suppose that a " union of souls " takes place between the two. And that is the goal of life. It is not common sense. It is rubbish. But it is traceably a product of the teaching of the Christian Church regarding marriage. Woman is an alluring but forbidden creature, by nature sinful, except when a mystical union, typifying that of Christ and his Church, has happened, thanks to priestly benediction.

The teaching of Islam is altogether different. There is no such thing as union of two human souls, and those who spend their lives in seeking it go far astray. Sympathy, more or less and love there may be. But every human soul is solitary from the cradle to the grave unless and until it finds its way of approach (wasîlah) to Allah. It is free and independent of every other human soul ; it has its full responsibility, must bear its own burden and find its own " way of approach " through the duties and amid the cares of life. There is no difference between the woman and the man in this respect. In marriage there is no merging of personalities; each remains distinct and independent. They have simply entered into an engagement for the performance of certain duties towards each other, an engagement which can be hallowed and made permanent by mutual regard and love. If that regard and love be not forthcoming the engagement had best be terminated. Marriage is not a sacrament—*i.e.*, of mystic value in itself—still less is it a bondage. It is a civil contract between one free servant of Allah and another free servant of Allah. Allah has ordained between them mutual love, has clearly defined their rights over one another, and has prescribed for their observance certain rules of honour and of decency. If they cannot feel the love, and fear they may transgress the rules, the contract should be ended. The woman retains her own complete personality, her own opinions and initiative, her own property and her own name, in the case of polygamic as of monogamic marriage; and in the case of polygamic marriage she can claim her own establishment. It, therefore, does not very greatly matter, from her point of view, whether monogamy or polygamy be the prevailing order of society.

The quasi-religious objection to the mere mention of polygamy to be met with in Europe today is owing to a preconception with regard to a marriage as a sacrament, a union in which woman makes the sacrifice of her identity. Monogamic marriage remains, as it has always been, the ideal of Islam, but it is recognised as an ideal only, which it really is. In practice, strict monogamy is a cause of much unhappiness and also of some serious social evils, which I have already mentioned. The law of Islam aims at happy marriage, so allowance is made for known human tendencies, and divorce is made quite easy where unhappiness can be shown to be the result of a particular marriage. This facility of divorce, which was not in the original Western code of monogamy, has now been introduced on grounds of reason and humanity in most Western countries. But it there involves so much publicity and scandal as to be almost in itself a social evil, which is certainly not the case with the Islamic method of divorce. I may add that happy marriage is not rarer among Muslims than it is among the peoples of the West.

Polygamy is not an institution of Islam. It is an allowance made for ardent human nature. The Qurân does not enjoin it, but recommends it in certain circumstances as better than leaving women helpless and without p᠆otectors. The permission is contained in the following verses, revealed at a time when the men of the small Muslim community had been decimated by war, and when there were many women captives, some with children clinging to them :

وآتـوا اليتـامي امـوا لهـم ولا تتبـدلوا الخبيث بالطيب ولا تاكلوا امـوالهـم الي امـوالـكم انـه كان حوبا كبيرا ـ وان خفتم الا تقسطوا في اليتامي فانكـحـوا ماطاب لـكم من النساء مثنيٍ وثلـث ورباع فان خفتم ان لا تعـدلوا فـواحدة اورماملكت ايـمـانـكم ذالـك

ادني ان لا تعولوا وآتوا النساء صدقاتهن نحلة
فان طبن لكم عن شيء منه نفسا فكلوه هنيئا مريئا .

"Give unto the orphans their wealth. Exchange not the valuable for the worthless (in your management thereof) nor absorb their wealth in your own wealth. Verily that would be great sin."

"And if ye fear that ye will not deal fairly by the orphans, then marry of the women (*i.e.*, their mothers) who seem good to you, two or three or four; and if ye fear that you cannot do justice (to so many) then one only or (of the female captives) whom your right hands possess. That is better, that ye stray not from the path of justice. And give unto the women (whom ye marry) free gift of their marriage portions; but if they, of their own accord, remit to you a part thereof, then ye are welcome to absorb it (in your wealth)."

The passage cannot, by any stretch of imagination, be made to fit in with the views so often ventilated by opponents of Islam. Polygamy is little practised in the Muslim world today, but the permission remains there to witness to the truth that marriage was made for man and woman, not man and woman for marriage.

Islam holds a man absolutely responsible for his treatment of every woman. Responsibility and decency are the pillars of Islamic ethics, and the arch which they support admits to liberty—the utmost liberty compatible with human happiness and welfare. The freedom of the West in this respect seems to us Muslims to have passed the bounds of decency ; which brings us to another much disputed point ; the separation of the sexes.

If it is true, as the experience of life suggests and the advocates of woman's rights in Europe and America are never tired of declaring that women's interests are separate from those of men, that women are really happier among themselves in daily life, and are capable of progress as a sex rather than in close subservience to men : then the Islamic rule which makes the woman mistress in her sphere is not in disaccord with human nature. While every provision is made for the continuation of the race, while the relation of a woman to her husband and near kinsfolk is just as tender and as intimate as in the West, the social life of woman is among themselves. There is no "mixed bathing", no mixed dancing, no promiscuous flirtation, no publicity. But according to the proper teaching of Islam there ought to be no bounds to woman's opportunities for self-development and progress in her sphere. There is nothing to prevent women from becoming doctors, lawyers, judges, preachers and divines, but they should graduate in women's colleges and practise on behalf of women.

Women may have their own great athletes, lawyers, physicians, scientists, and theologians ; and no true Muslim would withhold from them the necessary means of education in accordance with the Holy Prophet's own injunction. But if this very hopeful continent for human progress is to be explored successfully, there must be no mere sycophantic aping of the West. For the Western aspect of the question of feminine emancipation is quite different from the aspect which it bears among Islamic peoples. The women of the West have had themselves to agitate in recent years for simple legal rights, such as that of married women to own property, which have always been secured to women in Islam. They have had to wage a bitter fight to bring to the intelligence of Western men the fact that women's interests are not identical with those of men—a fact for which the Sacred Law makes full allowance. Women in the West have had to agitate in order to obtain recognition of their legal and civil existence, which was always recognised in Islam. They have now their own separate clubs which a Turkish lady visitor described as their "haram" or Zenâna quarters, which Muslim women in the central Muslim countries have always had in fact, if not in name. Therefore they started from a totally different point from that from which the Muslim women start. Their men secured the rights of women in Islam, and men will champion and secure what further rights they may require today in order to fulfil the spirit of the Sharî'ah. In this emancipation there will be no strife between the sexes. There is therefore really no analogy with the case of women in the West.

An objection is occasionally raised to the Islamic system on the ground that the parents choose a husband for the girl, who ought to be allowed to choose for herself. That social custom is not peculiar to Islam; it is the custom in many European countries; and in all countries, and among all peoples, it would be agreed that a young girl who chose a husband of whom her parents disapproved would be courting disaster. On the other hand no Muslim parent would ask his daughter to remain with a man whom she disliked. She would be taken home again. In Turkey,

where the circle of a grown-up girl's male acquaintance
has been enlarged so as to include relations of a marriage-
able degree, the daughter of a friend of mine informed her
father that she wished to marry Fulan Bey. Her father
said : " *Pek Iyi* (all right !). But you clearly understand that if you break through one old custom, you break
through all old customs which depend on it. If you
marry Fulan Bey, of whom I do not approve as a husband
for you—remember I know something of men and you
do not—you cannot come home to me in case of disagree-
ment and divorce, for I shall not receive you as I should
be bound by law and custom to do, if an unhappy marriage
had resulted from my choice for you. Take what I can
give you with my blessing, and go your way." The girl
gave in, deciding to be guided by her father's knowledge
and experience.

When Muslims think of feminine emancipation, the
Islamic ideal must always be kept in sight, or they will go
astray after something which can be no guide to them.
And at the same time we must remember—I say it again—
that the rules laid down by the Sacred Law are not static
but *dynamic* ; that the Sacred Law itself, the law of kindness, is greater than the rules laid down at any period,
that woman's rights increase with her responsibilities. The
Law of Islam for woman, as for man, is justice, the goal
of Islam is universal human brotherhood, which does not
exclude, but must include, the goal of universal sisterhood
as well. That goal can never be attained while the position of woman is what it is today in East or West.

EIGHTH LECTURE.

"THE CITY OF ISLAM."

I have hitherto been speaking to you chiefly of the past. I now, in this concluding lecture, wish to focus your attention chiefly on the present. I have shown that the standard of Islam in every sphere of human action, human intercourse, is certainly not lower than the highest standards of to-day. It is the Muslims who today fall short of the Islamic standard. I have explained the reasons, as I understand them, for the down-fall of the Muslim empire and decay of Muslim civilisation and I have told you how that downfall and decay, far from shaking the faith of Muslims in the Sharî'ah or Sacred Law, have strongly confirmed it. For they now see clearly that the cause of their humiliation has been neglect of some of the injunctions of the Sacred Law :

> "To obtain education is a religious duty for every Muslim, male and female."

> "Seek knowledge even though it be in China."

> "An hour's contemplation and study of God's creation is worth a year of adoration."

> "Trust in God but tie your camel,"

and many other sensible and plain commands. And Muslims now see clearly that the material success of Western nations is due to their adoption of that part of the Sharî'ah or Sacred Law of Islam which guards material progress and prosperity, and which the Muslims of the

11

decadence so foolishly neglected. Ideas and axioms the most abhorrent to the mind of Christendom when it was Christendom—I mean when the Christian Church dictated the ideas and practice of the Western peoples—but which were present in Islam from the beginning, and are embodied in the Sacred Law—have one by one, and gradually, become accepted by the people of the West. The duty of free thought and free inquiry; the duty of religious tolerance; the idea that conduct and not creed or class distinction must be the test of a man's worth in law and social intercourse; woman's right to full equality with man before the law, her right to property; the license to divorce and remarry; the duty of personal cleanliness; the prohibition of strong drink—all these well-known ingredients of the Sacred Law of Islam, which were all of them anathema to Christian Europe, and are still regarded by the Church as either irreligious or purely secular—that is, outside the purview of religion—have been incorporated in the ideology of Western civilisation. It can be proved, and has been proved by Christian writers, that all these modern ideas were derived from the Muslims of a bygone day. But they were, of course, adopted by the Europeans on the strength of the دليل العقلي (argument of reason) alone, not on the دليل الشرعي (the argument of divine sanction); which alone commended them at first to Muslims. The Muslims, from belief in their divine sanction, proceeded to a knowledge of the arguments of reason in favour of these ordinances. Is it possible that the West, having accepted them on the evidence of reason, may come eventually to belief in their divine sanction?

I hardly think so, until the West can come to recognise the divine sanction which is behind human reason; until the peoples come to know that all these things, which for the Christian rank as " secular," but which are of such vast importance to the welfare of mankind, form part, and only part, of an existing code of religious law, claiming to be of divine revelation; until they come to realise their need of the remaining portion of the Sharî'ah, the part which Muslims still hold fast, the part which guards political and social stability and progress. This the Muslims have held fast on the strength of the دليل الشرعى only for the past two or three centuries; but the دليل العقلي alone can bring non-Muslims to adopt it, and the دليل العقلي to-day is lacking in the only form in which it could appeal to the materially-minded a bright example of the whole Islamic polity in practice, upon modern lines.

We can show some notable achievements—the largest and most comprehensive human brotherhood the world has ever known, a society quite free from the internal strife and jealousy which threaten the existence of the Western social order, a practicable code of international law; a social code in which the claims of capital and labour, landlord and peasant, the rights of property and those of enterprise—nay, the very theories of monarchy, constitutionalism, socialism, communalism, aristocracy and democracy—are all quite happily reconciled. Yet, while there is no bright example of Islam in practice, in the shape of a successful and progressive modern state,

while the Muslim nations seem to be behind the Western
nations in material well-being, the latter will inevitably
turn away with the idea that the guiding principles of
such backward, unsuccessful peoples must of necessity be
inferior to their own. And they have every right to do
so, seeing what they see. The fault is ours, not theirs,
if the light of Islam is invisible to them.

Yet another thing which has confirmed the faith
of thinking Muslims in the Sharî'ah is the failure of
Western civilisation in the sphere of political and social
science in contrast to its wonderful success in natural
science—its utter failure so far to solve problems which
were settled centuries ago in Islam. We all agree that
it is desirable that the truths of Islam should be made
known and, as far as possible, commended to the modern
world. But some among us seem to think that the way
so to commend them is to disregard the Sharî'ah as something antiquated; and to present Islam as a religion
without a Law—a mere matter of personal belief, of
abstract thought and of detached opinion. Some Muslims,
rendered stupid by the onslaught of modern technical
efficiency, would be willing to accept not only the scientific
knowledge and achievements of the West—which Muslims
do most urgently require in order to complete the Sharî'ah
which has too long been mutilated—but also all the social
and political ideals and institutions of the West. That
is suicidal madness, as the Shahîd Sa'îd Halîm Pasha
warned the Muslims of the world in his remarkable work
in Turkish, "Islamlashmaq"; for the political and social
science of the West is, unlike the natural science of the

West, of haphazard growth and is based mainly not on demonstrable truths but on demonstrable fallacies. It is only the common sense of the English, their natural gift for making things unreasonable a success in practice, the mental energy and handiness their climate gives them which have enabled them to avoid a collapse, which has already come to other European countries, France (more than once), Russia, Italy. If the Muslims have declined through their neglect of certain portions of the Sharî'ah, that is no reason for discarding the remaining portions, but rather for restoring the whole and observing it with more intelligence. We want a clear code of the main principles and injunctions which can be placed in the hands of every Muslim, every Muslimah. At present, in existing works on Fiqh, we are confronted with the manifest absurdity that personal matters like the position in which the believer stands to pray, are made of equal importance with first principles, like the law forbidding murder. We have to distinguish once for all between that which is essential and of permanent homage value and that which was the currency of a particular historical period. Otherwise we are likely, most of us, to remain in the ignorant and bewildered state of men who cannot see the forest for the trees, who are so bothered with the emphasis on small particulars that they lose sight altogether of the motive and the goal. Muslims have everything to learn from Europe in the matter of natural science. They have nothing whatever to learn from Europe in the regions of political and social science. In such matters Islam found the way of peace thirteen centuries ago.

Christendom has not yet found it. The work before us is not, therefore, to discard Islamic institutions, putting Western institutions in their place, but to modernise Islamic institutions and uplift them to the present standard of efficiency.

Prince Sa'îd Halim, whom I knew well, was a man with practical experience of statesmanship in troublous times, well versed in modern European politics; a reformer and the son of a reformer; who had been forced by circumstances all his life to give much thought to problems concerning the future of Islam and of the Muslims; a man acquainted with the thought of England, France and Germany, as well as with the teaching of the Qurân and of the Holy Prophet, and the commentaries of the learned on that teaching. He was thus well qualified to advise the Muslim world as to its future policy, and his advice was not Auropalashmaq (Europeanise) but Islamlashmaq (Islamise). He had in mind an independent Muslim country which still retained some of the prestige of the historic Muslim Empire, and was still the seat of the Khilâfat. He, like the great majority of members of the Committee of Union and Progress, was a Khilâfatist. So, in his book, his aim was, first and foremost, to depict the true Islamic State in modern terms, and to contrast it with existing forms of Government. Such considerations do not so immediately concern the Indian Muslims as they did the Turks, but they are so interesting to us all that I shall give a brief account of them, with my own occasional comments, before proceeding to considerations of more immediate practical

use to us in India and more directly connected with my
previous lectures.

Prince Sa'îd Halim, in his task, had to overcome
difficulties which we shall not have to face, for it is no
easy business to translate the theory of Islamic Government as it existed in the time of the first four Khalifas
into modern terminology. The first four Khalifas, though
they ruled a mighty empire and though their armies and
their officers in all parts of the world paid absolute
obedience to their orders, had nothing in common with
despots, least of all with military despots. They led a
simple private life in Al-Madînah, not interfering at all
in the local government of the place, not interfering at all
with any local government so long as it did right. Their
words were absolute commands for all the Muslims;
but, except to the armies and to the officers entrusted
with the peaceful organisation of conquered regions,
they issued very few commands. They gave a plain
account of events and of their own executive actions in
the Khutbah every Friday in the Prophet's Mosque, and
were the ultimate appeal in all matters of religion, law
and government, and that was all. They were surrounded
by no pomp of an imperial court; they claimed no royal
reverence. Their private relations with the people of
Madînah and with all the Muslims who approached them
were quite frank and brotherly. When a poor old woman
rather rudely charged 'Umar ibn ul Khattâb with some
slight wrong to her, the people wished to push her away
but the Khalîfah ordered them to let her speak, saying :
" It is the duty of every Muslim and every Muslimah to

speak the truth to the ruler." All the Muslims knew the
Sacred Law and obeyed it; if they were in doubt they
went to the Khalîfah or his representative who solved
their difficulties for them in the simplest way. There
was no police, and no need of one. The liberties and self-
governing institutions of the people were secured, and the
Khalîfah's care was but to see that they enjoyed them.

A change came with the accession of Mûawwîyah
but it was not so great as has been generally represented,
for the principle of election was still respected in theory.
We find Muawwîyah the Second on his death-bed expressly
charging the people to elect the best among the Muslims
to succeed him—and the simplicity of the Arabs was
still maintained to some extent. If Bani Umâyyah had
given proof of their sincerity by refusing the succession
after Muawwîyah's death—it must be remembered that
they had a standing majority in Syria, Egypt, Northern
Arabia and North Africa and so could do as they like—
and electing the best of the Muslims from the point of
view of public service to succeed him, in the true Islamic
way, there could be no two opinions today as to the service
which they rendered to Islam, despite the crimes which
marked their rise to power. But after making ruthless
war on the dynastic party because of their desire to found
a dynasty—against the Holy Prophet's will, as Sunnis
hold—they themseves set up a dynasty, and thus de-
faced for us the outline of the perfect City of Islam. There
have been dynasties of the Khailâfat of Islam since then
until only the other day the last, inoffensive Khalîfah
of the illustrious House of Osmân was ordered out of
Turkey at a moment's notice.

There have been many good Muslims in the long line of Khalîfahs, and Islam has often flourished under them with something of its pristine brilliance, for the Shari'ah was always there to guide them in good Government. But one of the limits of Allah imposed on personal ambition was transgressed when the elective sovereignty for life was changed into hereditary sovereignty; and one of the safeguards of the pure theocracy was set aside. If the elective life-sovereignty of a peculiar kind, in conjunction with free local institutions and self-government (which I shall come to later) had endured till now, developed in accordance with the needs of the successive centuries, the task of reconstructing the Islamic State on modern line would have been comparatively simple, a mere question of reforms. As it is, there is a mighty gulf to bridge, from now to then, and Sa'îd Halîm Pasha does his best to bridge it for us. After this long digression, I now come to his ideas.

In the West to-day the chief position in the State is open to two sorts of persons only :—One who steps calmly into it by right of birth, whether fitted or unfitted to perform its duties, or one who is elected to it by the public voice. There would be nothing to be said against the latter course, from our theocratic standpoint, if the election were made deliberately from among the best, tried servants of the nation by a council of the wisest heads, and if the term of election were for life or for so long as the elected one governed rightly. But it is made haphazard by the fallacy that the majority is always right, and the vote is given to a multitude incompetent to judge aright in such a case. The persons from whom election is made are generally precisely those who, in wisdom, ought to be excluded altogether from the field of choice—men personally ambitious who are straining every nerve to rise to place and power. Among the early Muslims personal ambition—the desire of power for its own sake—was an absolute disqualification. Lest you should think that this old Islamic ideal of giving power to men who, like our Holy Prophet, have no lust of power—the only men who really ought to be allowed to hold it—is altogether lost among the Muslims of today, let me tell you that, in the first great organised movement for the revival of Islam on modern lines, that ideal was religiously observed. In the constitution of the Committee of Union and Progress it was laid down that personal ambition must be always in the servant's place. The chief executive power was confided to men who never came at all before the public, and the chief ostensible power to men who, already before the public, were the most indifferent to power, the most averse to pomp and ceremony; first to the martyr Mahmûd Shevket Pasha, and then to the martyr Sa'îd Halîm Pasha.

In the Muslim East today you will see that the dictators who have been elected are the men who have done greatest service to the nation, not men who have merely crushed a rival faction by the weight of an ephemeral majority. Contested elections form no part of Islamic institutions, for Islam has no belief in the collective infallibility of those who are individually incompetent, and it has no faith in the majority of the ignorant. Choice of the ruler is a serious matter which is entrusted only to wise heads acquainted with the personalities concerned. The Muslims, as a whole, have no part in the election. They simply ratify the choice or they denounce it. The head of the Muslim State is elected not for a short term only, but for life. He is invested with all powers of Government. In relation to the people he is an absolute monarch, but in relation to the Sharî'ah he is on a level with his poorest subject, he is merely a Muslim among Muslims, looking forward to the Day of Judgment when he will have to render an account of all his works. The people have no authority to get rid of him so long as he does right; but if he does wrong, the Sharî'ah itself gives them the right to call him to account and, if need be, depose him. In Western democratic States the vote of the people can depose a President who has done right—nay, can depose him even because he has done right and they prefer wrong. That would be quite impossible in the Islamic State, where there is a Law for ruler and for people in such matters.

Islam recognises no inherent rights of man as man. Rights are attached to functions, to duties properly performed, to knowledge and experience. That is to say there is no political or social right apart from competence. In the West, rights are recognised apart from competence. The most important rights of all, the right to vote on public questions, the right to legislate, the right to rule, are conceded to the utterly incompetent. Questions of the most delicate national importance are decided by the rough and tumble method of majority. The minority is in the position of a defeated enemy. It has no rights whatever, though it be composed of thoughtful men, against the majority, though it be composed of men intensely ignorant.

Majority and minority, in that sense, are unknown in the Islamic State. Here the popular assembly is not elected as in the West by constituencies which include all sorts of different interests, on the ground of party opinion; it is elected by constituencies composed of groups, such as trades, occupations, tribes and communities—which have essentially the same interests—on the ground of representative competence. Thus there is no opening for the tyrannising of majorities over minorities. And supposing that a majority holding a particular point of view did dominate the popular Assembly they could never tyrannise over the minority and their supporters throughout the country in the way in which majorities in power are wont to tyrannise in Europe—I mean, by legislation hostile to the minority's interests. For the popular Assembly, in the Muslim State, has no legislative function, or executive function. The executive function is vested solely in the ruler of the State, who appoints his delegates, and is responsible only to the Sharî'ah as represented by the Council of the Jurists, in whom the legislative function is entirely vested. New laws are made only by men learned in the guiding principles of law, men chosen by the popular assembly from among the multitude of those learned in the law on account of their enlightenment and understanding of the nation's needs. And legislation is a rare thing, not a daily occurrence. The laws of Islam are not passed in a heated assembly by men who ardently desire the legislation, in their interests, against men who as ardently oppose it, in their interests. The laws of Islam are firmly based upon the Sharî'ah and are therefore in the interests of the people as a whole. They are not the work of warring politicians, but of sober jurists. And they are not concerned with small matters of detail. The smaller matters, which in Europe go to Parliament, are here regulated by an order of the Executive.

We have seen revolutions in Europe. They result in the oppression of one sort of people by another, the only change being that it is a different sort of people who play the part of the oppressors after the revolution from that which played the part before. That is because the aim of one class or political party is not to enjoy equal rights with another, but to supplant and crush the other succeeding to all its privileges, including that of tyrannising; and because the goal pointed out to Man's ambition by the social and political text-books to the great examples of modern European history is that of irresponsible wealth and irresponsible power. In the same manner, we see nations seeking to ruin and destroy, or to enslave, each other. That is because the social and political order in Christendom is "بدون سلطان" ("Without divine authority"). It is devoid of an authority which all men recognise. It has behind it no effective sanction, such as the Sharî'ah provides for the Muslim social and political order. There is no general acknowledgment of a Higher Authority, a Higher Law, than those which man's ambition and brute force are able to establish temporarily. There are no generally respected limits except those imposed by force of circumstances; therefore there are no real safeguards for the social and political régime; nor can there be where folk are still in ignorance of the divine and natural laws on which the social and political structure must be based in order to acquire stability.

Europe was more advanced in this respect under the pre-Christian Roman Empire than it has ever been since Christianity prevailed, because the pagan Romans were concerned with this world, and the Church was not. The Romans cultivated some humanity and did not allow the doctrine of irresponsible power to go unchallenged practically, as the Church has done. They had a high official called Tribunus Plebis—The Tribune of the Common People—who had authority, and often used it to call the government to account on behalf of the people, even on behalf of individuals. Something of the Roman tradition revived in the Italian mediaeval republics, mixed with the free tradition of the younger races from the East which overran the Empire in the period of its decline. But it was as often as not opposed by the Christian Church, which, having taken to its heart the doctrine that the aim and object of religion is located in another world, far from establishing the ideal of God's actual Kingdom in this world—as Islam established it—often supported the doctrine of irresponsible power in the sphere which it regarded as " secular," and punished men who, like Savonarola, made bold to speak of the Kingdom of God as actual. The greatest thing that the Church ever did, that I can remember, to restrain the irresponsible

ambitions of the Christians was the institution of the
Trève Dieu—the truce of God—causing warfare to be
stopped on certain days of each year, which reminds
us of a similar institution among the Arabs of the time
of Ignorance; and that it forbade usury as strictly as
Islam forbids it.

Do not misunderstand me. The Christian Church
did much for the relief of misery and for the healing of the
wounds of Europe. It preached peace, but it preached
it at a distance from men's daily life, and pointed always
to the cloister as the road to heaven. It was thus remote
from life and frowned on life, an attitude which prevented
it from exercising an effectual check on the doctrine of
irresponsible power, even when some saintly men arose
who sought to do so. The Mediaeval Church, in general,
went with the times, and more often than not supported
the doctrine of irresponsible power. It was a son of the
Church in an especial sense, a natural son of Pope
Alexander VI, Cesare Borgia, who became, curiously
enough, the pattern of the Irresponsibles. This Cesare
or Caesar Borgia was the greatest tyrant of his time.
He was absolutely ruthless, but efficient. During his
ruthless pacification of the Abruzzi, part of the States of
the Church, he happened to be accompanied for some
time by an emissary of the Florentine Republic, one
Niccoló Macchiavelli who, disgusted with the disorders
which prevailed in his own free republic, was so struck by
the success of the fire-and-sword methods which he saw
employed by Cesare, that he beheld in utter ruthlessness
the best weapon of Government. Cesare is in fact the

hero of Macchiavelli's famous book " II Principe " (the Prince) which afterwards became the text-book of State Government for modern Europe—not only for despotic governments but democratic governments as well. The late Mr. Gladstone, reputed a great democrat and a religious man, accepts Macch avelli's " Prince " as his pattern in politics no less than does Frederick William of Prussia, or Catherine the Great. " The Prince " is the direct negation of Theocracy, for it acknowledges no power above the might of human government.

Similarly, there has been no steadfast ideal as a guide for social conduct and relations, the Christian Church upholding an ideal remote from actual life. Wealth and property have been, and are, held and administered without the limitations which a practical theocracy imposes. Generally, the down-trodden, envious of the privileges which the rich enjoy, aim at themselves attaining such wealth and privileges rather than at adjusting the balance. Thus there is no equilibrium and the philosophical politician, to soothe his conscience, talks of the swing of the pendulum, as if it were a regulated movement of a necessary part of a Machine; whereas it is the machine itself, the very structure of Society, which is swaying dangerously to and fro.

As for the Balance of Power, the famous European equilibrium, so often vaunted in Victorian days, it is altogether gone, now Central Europe lies in ruins. Is there anything in all this for anyone to copy ? least of all, people who have stable institutions of their own, covering the whole ground of sociology and politics ?

The terrific object-lesson of the last great war has led some thinkers to foresee that Western culture may destroy itself within a century by mere persistence in a course which has been proved disastrous. That the danger is realised by many people in Europe may be seen from the attempts to obviate it both before the war and after, by founding first a Hague Convention, then a League of Nations, and from the Labour Bureaux and Conciliation Boards which have sprung up so suddenly in every Western country. But the League of Nations and the Hague Tribunal are incapable of dealing effectively with the big sinners. They can only bring to book the sinners who are small and weak. Nothing really useful can be done without a complete change of ideal, without the recognition of a Higher Power and Authority than any which is founded on brute force. As a witty Frenchman once remarked: '*Si dieu n' existait pas il faudrait bien l'inventer.* (If God did not exist it would be necessary to invent Him). Western statesmen may have no belief in God, but they will have to act as if they believed in Him; they will have to accept the principles of Theocracy—the notion of a Higher Law than man's ambition, the unpalatable notion of a Day of Judgment—if they wish to rescue Europe and the world from a condition of perpetual danger.

In the social and political structure of Islam there is Authority which all must recognise. Behind every one of its institutions and ordinances there is a Sanction which all must reverence. To man's ambitions and devices real limits are imposed— حـدود الله) the limits of Allah), as they are called—boundaries which every Muslim must respect and admit himself in the wrong if he transgresses one of them. These are the safeguards of the rights of men and nations. In the Islamic polity there are no such ideas as irresponsible power, or irresponsible wealth, or irresponsible government, or irresponsibility of any kind. Power and wealth are limited by man's admitted and accepted responsibility to Allah, and the manner of their use is prescribed in the Sacred Law. In commercial dealings there are limits: the respect for contracts and a man's pledged word, the prohibition of usury and gambling. On private dealings there are limits, and on individual conduct, such as the prohibition of intoxicants, the laws concerning kind and equitable treatment of women, justice to servants, charity to poor relations and the strict law governing inheritance: " No testament to the detriment of heirs is lawful." There are very salutary limits to the relations of capital and labour or employer and employed. " Wealth properly employed," said the Prophet (may God bless and keep him) —that is, wealth spent in strict accordance with the Sharī'ah —" is a blessing (to the world at large) ; and a person may lawfully endeavour to increase it by honourable means." (i.e., not by usury or any kind of oppression.)

> " A tax must be taken from the rich and distributed among the poor."

> " He is no true Muslim who eateth his fill, and leaveth his neighbour hungry."

> " Pay the labourer his hire before his sweat drieth."

There are limits imposed on warfare, such as respect for treaties, the order not to destroy the enemy's means of subsistence, respect for non-combatants, the order to show mercy to the surrendered enemy, and so on, as I have already shown. There are limits imposed on diplomacy, and on every form of national aggression:

"He is not one of us who sides with his tribe in oppression, nor is he one of us who calls others to assist him in injustice, nor is he one of us who dies while assisting his tribe in tyranny."

That was a limit which resulted in the total disappearance of aggressive nationalism in all the countries which profess Islam. You may think it odd that I should say this at a time when nationalism appears to be rampant in the Muslim world, when we read of Turkish nationalism, Egyptian nationalism, Syrian nationalism, Mesopotamian nationalism. The nationalism to be found in Muslim lands today is all defensive or protective as against European aggressive nationalism—or imperialism, which is merely aggressive nationalism fully grown—not against other Islamic nationalisms. Indeed it is marked by a new warmth of Muslim brotherhood. This abolition of aggressive nationalism, with the brotherhood of every race and class and colour in the body of Islam, is perhaps the greatest actual achievement we can show today, when the limits are no longer perfectly observed, when the bulwarks of the theocracy are in places broken down, though not irreparably.

It was those limits which preserved Islamic civilisation intact through revolutions such as marked the rise and fall of Bani Ummâyah and the passing of the Khilâfat from one great Muslim racial group to another; through catastrophes like the invasion of Chenghiz Khan, down even to the present day. For it is still essentially intact: make no mistake about that. The Sharî'ah is still the Sacred Law for all the nations who profess Islam. The Turks, in their reforms, appeal to it at every step, and the reactionaries here appeal to it when opposing all reforms. The Muslim Bolsheviks (so called) of Russia claim no more for Bolshevism than that, as they conceive and experience it, it is not against the Sharî'ah. The aim of every Muslim is to restore the Sharî'ah in its first purity, translated into terms of modern life. We differ only as to details of interpretation and as to the methods which should be employed.

It was those limits—though occasionally far from perfectly observed—which caused millions of Christians, Jews, Zoroastrians, Hindus, Buddhists and Confucians to be tolerated and protected, often honoured, in the Muslim Empire through all the centuries when Europe thought it a religious duty to destroy non-Christians. It was those limits which made the Turks, when fighting for the bare existence of their country at Gallipoli, refuse to use the poison gas the Germans offered them. It is those limits which have kept before the Muslims, even under most despotic governments, the ideal of universal human brotherhood; and have preserved the Muslim polity from the evils of aristocracy, plutocracy and democracy, while diffusing aristocratic virtues and democratic freedom of intercourse throughout the whole community.

Is it wonderful that we Muslims still believe, and believe more firmly than ever, in our theocratic institutions; and that we see in them the way of escape from the perilous social and political confusion and uncertainty which co-exists with material well-being in the modern civilisation of the West; the only way to get rid of the hatred between classes and nations, to soften the clash of diverse aims and traditions, by bringing the Monarchist, the Constitutionalist, the Socialist, the Syndicalist and the Communist into the same world of ideas—in other words, to save modern civilisation (which after all belongs to all of us, as being the highest civilisation of the age in which we live) from the destruction from within which plainly threatens it ? 'In Islam it is of no very great importance whether the Government is an elected sovereignty for life, or a hereditary sovereignty, despotic or constitutional, or a republic, or even a Soviet republic, provided that the Sharî'ah remains supreme.

The principle points of Prince Sa'îd Halîm's presentment of the modern Islamic state may be thus summarised. The distinction between secular and religious in matters of administration, education, policy and general dealing has no right whatever to exist in the Islamic State. Where God is King the secular becomes religious. All that would remain would 'be persons specially learned in matters of religion, the reverence paid to whom would be entirely owing to their knowledge as displayed in actual work from among their number the members of the Legislative body would be elected by the people's representatives. In short, the first thing to be done is to get rid altogether of that "pseudo-priesthood" to which Sa'îd Halîm refers as the Chief Misleader of the Muslim World. The State itself. heaving been "Islamised" and organised upon the lines I have already indicated, and having the advice of experts in Islamic ethics, politics and sociology, who alone possess the right (due to their competence) to frame new laws, will proceed on lines consistent with the basic principles of the Sharî'ah such as :

Equality of all individuals, male and female, before the law.

Universal education both of males and females.

Absolute religious tolerance.

Prohibition of usury (which means that it is unlawful for a Muslim to derive or seek to derive profit from the misfortune of a fellow-man). Thus in the Islamic State, measures would be taken to stop profiteering in the necessaries of life, as well as usury properly so called.

Prohibition of the sale of alcoholic drink.

Prohibition of gambling.

The institutions of Zakât and the Beyt-ul-Mâl, which secure a fair distribution of wealth throughout the community.

Respect for the rights of property within the limits laid down by the Sacred Law.

The Sanctity of all contracts.

The institution of marriage as a civil contract between free individuals, with facilities for divorce and remarriage which without undue publicity or the need for any scandal, allow to men and women in such matters the utmost liberty compatible with decency, with the welfare of both sexes, and with the rights of children.

The maintenance of a decent reserve between the sexes, for the safety of women.

The Islamic law of Inheritance, which prevents undue accumulation of wealth by individuals and secures a portion of it to the women of a family.

Respect for women's persons, property and rights.

Respect for the rights of children, particularly of orphan children, and recognition of the State's responsibility towards them.

Universal military training as distinct from conscription.

The Islamic regulations concerning foreign policy. Sanctity of treaties, prohibition of aggressive nationalism and aggressive warfare.

Strict observance of the Islamic laws of war (if war unhappily should be forced on the Islamic State by the aggression of others), respect for all non-combatants and for the means of livelihood of the enemy: the use of no weapon which has not already been used against the Muslims by the enemy; mercy and forgiveness to the con uered.

I think that this is what may be truly described as an " advanced " programme for any modern State.

I have been led by my interest in Prince Sa'îd Halîm's speculations to dwell, perhaps, too long upon an aspect

of the question which is hardly presented to us for solution.
Here in India we are not concerned with reconstituting
the Islamic Sovereign State—which was Prince Sa'îd
Halîm's most pressing concern—but with restoring a
sadly decayed Muslim community living together with
other co mmunities under a system of Government which
allows plenty of scope for such a restoration and revival.
Here we are not concerned with the manner of the election
of the ruler, with the constitution of the national assembly
and the Council of the 'Ulama but rather with the great
basic principles of the Sharî'ah and with those local
institutions which have existed almost unimpaired in
Muslim countries from the time of the first rightly-guided
Khalîfahs until now—though they have not existed unimpaired in India.

My casual reading of Indian History leads me even
to doubt whether true Islamic institutions have ever
existed in India at all. But they exist elsewhere and are
quite easily retraceable.

The first thing that you have to do is to remove the
curse of ignorance, which is the root cause of the degradation of the Muslims at present. Islam does not admit of
ignorance, and where ignorance prevails Islam is not. It
is not a religion of superstition and priestcraft which,
fungus-like, can thrive in darkness and in foul surroundings. It is the religion of free air and daylight, the religion
of the truth of God's creation. Islam, as planted in the
world, needs all available light and knowledge for its
growth. We have to secure to every Muslim man and
woman access to all the available light and knowledge of

the present day. Education must be universal, and it must be Muslim education. It must not treat all practical and material knowledge as " secular " and apart from religion, but it must do as did the Muslim universities of old, and make all learning religious; it must give to all learning " a place in the Mosque." There is nothing in the science of the present day that Muslims need be afraid of. It is in fact the outcome and continuation of the science of the Muslims in the great days of Islamic culture. It is not against the proper teaching of Islam, but is included in it. Your village mosques should be your village schools and your great mosques in cities should be your universities. Let the instruction given be as modern as you please, it still comes within the scope of Al-Islam, if Muslims will but wake up to perception of that fact. In the mosque, according to the ancient practice, anyone may give a course of lectures who is competent to teach the subject, and we have many educated men in the country who could not practise a more noble or more truly Muslim form of charity than this of bringing knowledge to the ignorant. The first Islamic duty is to dispel the cloud of ignorance which dulls the intellect of so many of our brethren, and harbours so much evil for Islam and India.

The revival of Islamic science, art and literature will follow on the liberation of men's minds. I need not speak about it separately, for it has no separate importance.

Never forget that Muslims are brothers, and that the ordinances of our religion—I mean, our religion as the

Holy Quran and the Holy Prophet entrusted it to our keeping, not as it is represented by some folks today— are meant to bind together and preserve that brotherhood. Do not be led astray by anything or any one to regard those ordinances as meaningless or out of date. They are only meaningless if the brotherhood of Islam has become a dead letter ; and they are not out of date since the need of universal human brotherhood, with a code of rules to guard it, was never more apparent than it is today. The five daily prayers, the pilgrimage, the fast of Ramadhan, quite apart from their benefit to the individual worshipper, are witnesses to the brotherhood of all nations and languages and classes and castes.

And if you really wish to restore the Islamic community and give it vigorous growth, you must absolutely re-establish the collection and distribution of زَكوة and must confide it to the wisest and most upright men in every town and district; who would use it, as it should be used, to discourage idleness and begging and vice, and to foster the ideal of honest independence in our poorer brethren.

Avoid even the shadow of usury in all transactions between Muslims. I am aware that the financial and commercial systems of the present differ materially from those of the past. The Holy Qurân allows trade but forbids usury. Now usury means taking an unfair advantage of a brother's need, and trade means supplying a brother with that which he requires at a just price. That undoubtedly is the Quranic meaning of the terms. I think myself that much of modern commerce does not fall under the Quranic " trade " at all, but under usury. And I know that many Muslims hold that certain kinds of loans for interest, usual nowadays, are not usurious, becasue they do not injure any fellowman. It may be so, but from the point of view of human brotherhood all such transactions are undesirable. The general social influence of the present system is, upon the whole, against fraternity. Why is it that the abolition of interest is in the forefront of every Socialist programme ? Why was it that when Communism came to power in Russia the first thing that it did was to abolish interest, and the whole system which admits it ? It is because the capitalist order of society—already threatened with destruction everywhere in Europe after barely a century of existence— is based on usury, and because that, in the opinion of the thinkers opposed to it, is the reason why it is productive of so much social injustice. Therefore, for the sake of our fraternity I say : Avoid even the shadow of usury in transactions between Muslims. If the shadow must fall on us, let it be only in transactions with other communities with whom usury is an established institution and then let it be only what is absolutely necessary for the discharge of ordinary business. If Muslims must not receive interest, neither should they pay interest. Therefore they must not borrow from people of other communities, and the proper Muslim organisation must be re-established for helping them at times of real need. The same organisation would serve to discourage loans for purposes of senseless ostentation or extravagance, and so check one of the chief causes of the economic weakness of the Indian

Muslims. For improving the economic status of the community and at the same time safeguarding our Islamic brotherhood—the two aims would be incompatible if we blindly followed European methods—you will find everything that you require in the old Islamic system of finance, and I advise you strongly to devote some study to it.

Enforce the prohibition of strong drink and gambling with all the weight of our social and personal influence.

Be strict in observance of the Islamic Law of inheritance.

Wage war on ignorance, keep to your Islamic duties. Re-establish regular payment of زكوة , restore the Beyt-ul-Mal. And you will soon have a decent, prosperous, advanced, well-organised community instead of the mere rabble which we see at present.

I have spoken to you of the charge of fatalism as a charge unjustly brought against Islam. It is unjustly brought against Islam, but not unjustly brought against large numbers of the Muslims. In the ignorant masses there is found a blind and stupid fatalism, simply because they are ignorant and know little or nothing of Islam. It comes from the mistaken notion of Jihâd—the effort every Muslim is obliged to make—as limited to war against unbelievers; whereas war against unbelievers is nowhere enjoined, but war against evil, war against aggressive wrong, war on behalf of right, war against idleness and sloth and lethargy and dirt and ignorance is everywhere enjoined and in every vocation of life, even in a man's own home, even in a man's own soul. Jihâd is the whole life of the true Muslim, and when his whole life is illuminated and ennobled by the spirit of Jihâd then indeed he has a right to be a fatalist to this extent; that, aware that he is doing his duty with all his might at all times, he has no care for anything that may befall him, he trusts to the word of Allah:

ولا خوف عليهم ولاهم يعــزنــون .

" There shall no fear come upon them, neither shall they suffer grief."

If Islam is to be commended to the modern world Muslims must display again the spirit of Jihâd in every walk of life, must strive unceasingly for what they believe to be right against what they believe to be wrong, and so gain the respect which the Muslims of old gained. Their conduct and their conduct only can commend Islam and its institutions to the other peoples of the earth. We cannot adopt the institutions of any other people in place of our own, though we may, after due consideration, adopt some institutions in addition to our own. The Muslims must be organised as Muslims, or, they must lose the strength of their complete theocracy which is the greatest contribution which they have to offer to the modern world. There is nothing here in India to prevent them from organising themselves on Muslim lines and developing their own institutions to the highest point of strength and efficiency.

For organisation, the Muslims of all India might be represented by a council of the wisest heads in all matters

which concern the whole community, such as Muslim
education, and the co-ordination of the local efforts for
revival and reform. And each group and district should
have its own representative system upon Muslim Lines.
And here we come again to the Islamic State, but to the
lower and internal parts of its machinery, not the upper
parts which Sa'îd Halîm Pasha reconstructed. In the
Islamic State the constituency is made as small as possible
in order that all the constituents may be well acquainted
with the representative whom they elect from among
themselves; and it is composed of people of the same,
and not conflicting, opinions and interests, so that he may
fairly represent all of them. You may say that, in that
case, we should have innumerable Members of Parliament.
I am not talking of members of Parliament but of the
members of the lowest representative body, the council
of the trade or occupation in the town, and the village
council in the country. Each of those lowest representative bodies elects a representative from among its
members, and those elected representatives together form
the city council or the district council, which in turn
elects from among its members a representative for a
provincial council, and so on up to the popular Assembly,
or Council of State, as it was sometimes called.

This is quite different from the parliamentary system,
but it has its manifest advantages. For instance, the
whole constituency is, in each case, thoroughly competent
to elect, and the men to be elected to the higher councils
are only such as have proved their fitness for election, and
have some experience. This is the old Oriental system of

self-government—the system of shuyûkh or headmen—consecrated by Islam. And, as far as I know, it has never failed to prove effective when allowed to operate with reasonable freedom in any Eastern land. It has the great advantage of affording honourable advancement to men of solid worth, men who have worked hard all their lives for public causes, without any of the claptrap of the demagogue. I commend it to you as the proper system of representation for Muslims, in their communal organisation, to adopt.

I have told you very plainly what I think about the present general position of Muslim women in India. It must be improved. Education must be given them in accordance with our Holy Prophet's own express command, and they must be given scope for the development of the much good which Allah has placed in them. They have the same right as men to full development, and those who withhold that right from them are doing a great wrong.

Muslims cannot adopt the institutions of other communities, but it is their duty to respect the customs and institutions of other communities, and to live with them on terms of neighbourly regard and tolerance. Intolerance and what is called fanaticism have nothing to do with the religion of Islam. The Holy Quran and the example of the Holy Prophet forbid intolerance, and even the least discourtesy to people of another faith. Intolerance in professed Muslims can only come from ignorance of Islam. And the height of intolerance to be found in India only indicates the depth of ignorance to be found in India. We want the presence of the Muslim community to be an evident blessing to all the peoples of India, not a curse; and so the need for education becomes more urgent. The horror and the shame of the intolerance must have been brought home lately to everyone—as it was brought home most poignantly to me—by the murder of a man whom I respected very highly. There is nothing in the teaching of Islam to justify hatred of any man for his opinions or for seeking to win others to his opinions. God forbid that I should have to say it: There is nothing in the teaching of Islam to justify murder. Islam preaches equal justice to all men, tolerance for all sincere opinions, respect for all good men, wherever found. Islam is not against the rest of the world, but for the rest of the world, striving for right wherever found against wrong wherever found. I would urge most strongly on your notice the need to preach and practice ceaselessly this virtue of Islamic tolerance. We are forbidden to upset the wine of the non-Muslim. We are forbidden to speak anything concerning his religion which could hurt his feelings. The tolerance of Islam in history is our great claim to the consideration of the world. The tolerance of Islam in the future may heal the wounds of humanity. Let that tolerance be established, and if need be, enforced among you in the present. Here again is need for organisation and for discipline.

Many professed Muslims speak today exactly as the Jews and Christians spoke in our Holy Prophet's time, as if none but members of their own community could enter paradise.

ان الذين آمنـوا والـذين هـادوا والنصارى
والصابئين من آمن بالله واليوم الاخر وعمل صالحا
فلهم اجرهم عنـد ربهم ولا خـوف عليهـم ولا هـم
يحـزنون ·

" Verily, those who believe and those who keep
the Jew's religious rule, and Christians, and
Sabaeans—whoever believeth in Allah and the
Last Day, and doeth right—Surely their reward
is with their Lord, and there shall no fear come
upon them, neither shall they suffer grief."

And again :

وقالـوا لـن يـد خـل الـجـنـة الا مـن كان هـودا
او نصارى تلك امانيهـم قل هـا تـوا برهانـكم ان كنتم
صادقين - بلي من اسلم وجهـه لله وهـو محسن فلـه
اجره عنـد ربـه ولا خـوف عليهـم ولاهم يحـزنون ·

" And they say : None entereth paradise except
he who is a Jew or a Christian. These are their
own desires. Say : Bring your proof (of that
which ye assert) if ye be truthful.

" Nay, but whosoever surrendereth his purpose to
Allah while doing good (to men) surely his
reward is with his Lord; and there shall no fear
come upon them, neither shall they suffer grief."